P9-DOF-941

ALSO BY SAM ROBERTS

Grand Central: How a Train Station Transformed America

America's Mayor: John V. Lindsay and the Reinvention of New York (editor)

*Only in New York: An Exploration of the World's Most Fascinating,
Frustrating and Irrepressible City*

A Kind of Genius: Herb Sturz and Society's Toughest Problems

Who We Are Now: The Changing Face of America in the 21st Century

The Brother: The Untold Story of the Rosenberg Case

Who We Are: A Portrait of America Based on the Latest U.S. Census

The New York Times Reader (editor)

*"I Never Wanted to be Vice-President of Anything!":
An Investigative Biography of Nelson Rockefeller* (with Michael Kramer)

A
HISTORY OF
NEW YORK
IN
101
OBJECTS

· SAM ROBERTS ·

SIMON & SCHUSTER

New York   London   Toronto   Sydney   New Delhi

Simon & Schuster
1230 Avenue of the Americas
New York, NY 10020

Copyright © 2014 by Sam Roberts

All rights reserved, including the right to reproduce this book or portions thereof in any form whatsoever. For information address Simon & Schuster Subsidiary Rights Department, 1230 Avenue of the Americas, New York, NY 10020.

First Simon & Schuster hardcover edition September 2014

SIMON & SCHUSTER and colophon are registered trademarks of Simon & Schuster, Inc.

For information about special discounts for bulk purchases, please contact Simon & Schuster Special Sales at 1-866-506-1949 or business@simonandschuster.com.

The Simon & Schuster Speakers Bureau can bring authors to your live event. For more information or to book an event contact the Simon & Schuster Speakers Bureau at 1-866-248-3049 or visit our website at www.simonspeakers.com.

Interior design by Joy O'Meara
Jacket design by Marlyn Dantes
Jacket photographs (top to bottom): arrowhead © American Museum of Natural History; statue © Niko Koppel; World Trade Center dust © New-York Historical Society; keg from Erie Canal © New-York Historical Society; badge © Tony Cenicola/Redux Pictures; Phantom of the Opera mask © Tony Cenicola/Redux Pictures; yellow cab © Image Source/Corbis; bagel © Lisa Larson-Walker; coffee cup © Tony Cenicola/Redux Pictures

Manufactured in the United States of America

1 3 5 7 9 10 8 6 4 2

Library of Congress Control Number: 2013050297
ISBN 978-1-4767-2877-3
ISBN 978-1-4767-2880-3 (ebook)

"I.G.Y. (What a Beautiful World)." Words and music by Donald Fagen. Copyright © 1982 Freejunket Music (ASCAP). All rights reserved. Used by permission.

"This Land Is Your Land." Words and music by Woody Guthrie. WGP & TRO-© Copyright 1956 (Renewed) 1958 (Renewed) 1970 (Renewed) 1972 (Renewed) Woody Guthrie Publications, Inc. & Ludlow Music, Inc., New York, NY. Administered by Ludlow Music, Inc. Used by Permission.

To Dylan and Isabella

It is only in the world of objects that we have time and space and selves.

—*T. S. Eliot*

• Contents •

• Introduction •

A teddy bear or other childhood totem. That game-winning high school football. A Beatles concert ticket stub from Shea Stadium. The fraternity pin from you-know-who. A grandchild's first tooth. Your retirement watch from work.

Imagine having to choose just one object that defined your life.

Which one would it be?

Searching for paradigmatic but quirky artifacts that define the past is an irresistible parlor game. A few years ago, the British Museum and BBC Radio compiled *A History of the World in 100 Objects.* When I played a local version for *The New York Times,* though, their 100-object cap proved too confining. Call it a conceit, but doing justice to the history of a city this big took 101.

The criteria for this kaleidoscopic *History of New York in 101 Objects* were not arbitrary. My choices—from an artichoke to an elevator safety brake, a public high school yearbook to a cheap handgun, a skeletal model of King Kong sans rabbit fur to a mechanical cotton picker—were highly subjective. The objects themselves had to have played some transformative role in New York City's history or they had to be emblematic of some historic transformation. They also had to be enduring, which meant they could not be disproportionately tailored to recent memory or contemporary nostalgia. Fifty, or even twenty-five years from now, would they seem as vital or archetypal as they do right now? "The closer you get to the *now*, the more objects you can think of, but their longevity is harder to get a sense of," Dr. Jeremy D. Hill, the British Museum's research manager, told me. "When the British public was asked to nominate objects for our list, the vast majority were only one generation old. But in two hundred years' time, how many of these would you choose to be talking about?"

That meant leaving out lots of twenty-first-century objects—from Volume I, at least.

The British Museum and other institutions that have compiled similar lists generally limited themselves to items in their own collection. We imposed no such boundaries—only that an object could not be a human being, alive or dead (Mayor Ed Koch, who died in 2013, got the most nominations from *Times* readers). Nor too much bigger than a breadbox (which ruled out Central Park, the Empire State Building, the Statue of Liberty, the Parachute Jump, Washington Square Arch, the Staten Island Ferry, and the Unisphere, among many others). The object had to have existed someplace and at some time and still survive in some form (only one in our list could not be found). Our objects could come from any place, but they had to illuminate great New York movements or great moments, personify individuals who played an outsize role in the city's development, or typify epochal transmutations in its ongoing metamorphosis.

With those goals in mind, the 101 objects in this book were winnowed from hundreds of possibilities.

People and events shape history, but do inanimate doodads? Recently, in writing a book about Grand Central Terminal, I learned that even a single building could be transformational. Grand Central epitomized a convulsion in civil rights, communication, landmarks preservation, and urban planning—the terminal shifted Manhattan's cultural center of gravity to its very doorstep. By weaving its way into the fabric of American culture, this majestic beaux arts monument to civic and corporate pride embodied the soul of the city and a locus of new beginnings.

Still, a building is one thing—even one located in "Skyscraper National Park," as Kurt Vonnegut called Manhattan. Can a single *object* affect, much less make, history? Of course. Where would we be without the wheel, much less a crucifix or a credit card (Brooklyn is the "Borough of Churches," and the first bank charge card was invented there in 1946). "You can find the entire cosmos lurking in its least remarkable objects," Wisława Szymborska, the Polish poet, wrote. This book is a biography of material things—things, some remarkable, some mundane, that eloquently objectify and illuminate history through their own unique prism. They may be inanimate, but they have taken on lives of their own.

These 101 begin before history, hundreds of millions of years ago, when geology created the physical contours that made New York a natural harbor and downtown and midtown an unshakable foundation for manmade objects, ranging from the metallic spires of soaring skyscrapers to doughy bagels dense enough to be doorstops. The bedrock amphibolite, Fordham gneiss, and Manhattan schist forged by volcanic upheavals weathered millennia. But as Neil MacGregor, the director of the British Museum, observed, "A history through objects can never itself be fully balanced because it depends entirely on what happens to survive."

While the earliest objects are in short supply, I try to trace the First Peoples in what became New York, displaced by the early Dutch settlers, whose pragmatic tolerance for diversity distinguished the colony from English, French, and Spanish settlements (but did not rule out kidnapping and enslaving Africans). A century of British rule climaxed in seven years of largely forgotten but miserable occupation by enemy troops during the American Revolution and then a fateful, cunning political calculation to shift the new nation's capital to a swamp in the South.

The nineteenth century witnessed gargantuan growth, fueled largely by European immigration and industrialization, which elevated New York into the nation's manufacturing and maritime capital (and shaped its ambivalence about the Civil War) and, by the beginning of the next century, into its gilded cultural capital, too. In the twentieth, New York also became the capital of the world. As the new millennium neared, the city struggled on the brink of bankruptcy and chaos, but it survived a baptism by fire to begin the twenty-first century stronger and more vibrant than ever.

• • •

I consulted colleagues, museum curators, librarians, historians, archivists, novelists, experts and novices, friends and total strangers for what began as a search for fifty representative objects (constrained by the space requirements of print in *The New York Times*). Fifty wasn't enough. In a follow-up article, I incorporated fifteen more, culling them from suggestions by hundreds of readers who weighed in.

Those objects and the dozens more in this expanded book version define us in surprising ways. They range from distinctive curios you didn't know existed to prosaic artifacts that we take for granted but are unmasked in a different light. Valuing diversity, we encompassed the broad spectrum of human experience, perhaps at the expense sometimes of the obvious. (As Dr. Hill recalled, "There's a limit to the number of stone axes or Buddhas one can include.") Not all the searches were productive. One proved particularly vexing: how to illustrate a negative, the city's dramatic decline in crime since the 1990s—an intact pane of glass to prove the broken-window theory of policing? (Suggestions welcome!)

My original goal was to be provocative. I succeeded. How, readers demanded, could I have included a MetroCard but not a subway token? What about the Spaldeen? A woman in Tokyo suggested those singular orange-and-white Con Ed steam chimneys. Why a black-and-white cookie (author's prerogative: I crave them) but not a knish or an egg cream or a pizza slice or an artisanal microbrewed beer or a soggy hot dog purchased from a sidewalk vendor under a blue and yellow umbrella? After all, New Yorkers *are* what they eat. Food preoccupied people more than any other single category, leading me to suggest that Richard Castellano's immortal words from *The Godfather* be enshrined as New York's unofficial motto. If Chicago's is "Where's Mine?," New York's, particularly in an era of plummeting crime, deserves to be: "Leave the gun. Take the cannoli."

• • •

We all bring predispositions to our choices and our criteria. One of mine was to be unconventional, to leave both of us—me and you, the reader—surprised by what we just learned, or inspired to suggest some even more appropriate exemplar. The goal was not to be deliberately obscure but to be revealing by whimsically heading down some less traveled avenue (or, more likely, a barely tramped footpath) toward a historical imperative.

We tend to be preoccupied by the present, with one eye cocked on the future.

But history, after all, isn't really about the past. Our history is about who we are right now and where, as a society, we're headed (just as an obituary isn't about death but about a life). The goal is "effective history"—history that informs the present, that helps understand New York and how New Yorkers understand themselves.

"You could grow up in the city where history was made," Jonathan Lethem wrote in *The Fortress of Solitude*, "and still miss it all." Think of this, then, as a road-less-traveled guidebook to what you may have missed.

• • •

Like the original version, even this expanded list constitutes *a* history of New York—not *the* history. It's actually *my* history, an idiosyncratic exploration of New York exceptionalism by a journalist who has been covering the city for nearly fifty years and whose specialty seems to have become turning history into front-page news. I did that a few years back with the first recorded murder in New York—four hundred years ago—and with the unreported shrinking of a monumental skyscraper, by recalling the first black police officer and the restoration of a tombstone for the author of the nation's first Yiddish cookbook.

Any definitive history, as the British Museum's MacGregor acknowledged, would have been an "absurdly ambitious" quest. His list included the Rosetta Stone, of course. Maybe our seventeenth-century Dutch-English dictionary is comparable. But think of this entire book as a literary version of the Rosetta Stone—a template for translating, reimagining, and reinterpreting a history you thought you knew and for conjuring up other objects that were equally transcendent. This is a book for people who love New York—or love to hate it. Who can't get enough of the things that make us New Yorkers.

• • •

As much as this list is geocentric, it is not just a history of New York. A reader from North Carolina said he welcomed it as an antidote to "the New England–centered standard history of our country." The diversity reflected by my original list of objects, he wrote, implies or expresses "themes which are New York's continuing legacy to our nation."

Kenneth T. Jackson, the Columbia University historian, likes to say that America begins in New York. The Erie Canal not only established the city's maritime supremacy; it exported its culture and politics. The consolidation of the city inspired similar conglomerations. Innovations originally unique to New York spread rapidly to other metropolitan areas across the country because they were too transformative to be contained in a single city of infinite possibilities, even the nation's biggest.

"New York is to the nation what the white church spire is to the village," E. B. White wrote, "the visible symbol of aspiration and faith, the white plume saying the way is up!"

Among the objects suggested by readers was Walt Whitman's 1855 *Leaves of Grass*, which itself contains a fitting coda to any finite list of influential objects: "I am large," Whitman wrote in "Song of Myself." "I contain multitudes."

A
HISTORY OF
NEW YORK
IN
101
OBJECTS

·1·

Fordham Gneiss

Where the Skyscrapers Are

Dense, dark green to black, banded, grainy-textured, it punctuates the unseen underbelly of Manhattan. It was formed hundreds of millions of years ago in a crucible of immense heat and pressure, a tectonic upheaval as volcanoes erupted and the continental plates of Pangaea, the supercontinent, ground against each other. They divided, creating a vast gulf that would separate the Eastern Seaboard from North Africa. It is a rock. It is an island.

Manhattan is a geologist's dream. But sophisticated on-site analysis of what lies beneath the surface is a relatively recent phenomenon. Construction of Water Tunnel No. 3, as deep as six hundred feet below street level, the Second Avenue Subway, the Flushing Line Subway Extension, and the Long Island Rail Road's East Side Access project to Grand Central Terminal under Park Avenue opened a basement window for geologists to confirm their vision of how Manhattan was formed and why skyscrapers sprouted downtown and in midtown but not in between.

Depending on where you live in Manhattan, you can't honestly say it's not your fault. What geologists found was a wide variety of metamorphic rock—formed as tectonic plates collided—and distinct geological fault lines along Dyckman Street,

125th Street, Morningside Drive, and Canal Street, suggested by water coursing through the paths of least resistance, fractures and fissures that reached across the spine of Manhattan between the East and Hudson Rivers. While Manhattan schist is the best known of the rock formations that form the city's subbasement, the island is also defined by amphibolite, by Inwood marble farther uptown, and by Fordham gneiss, which predominates in the Bronx, on Roosevelt Island, and on the Lower East Side (and protruding on "C-rock" opposite the Columbia University athletic complex).

Gneiss (pronounced "nice") dates back a dazzling 1.2 billion years, when earth-shattering continental collisions caused sedimentary rock to recrystallize into contorted black-and-white-banded metamorphic rock. It is the oldest natural New York object. (The oldest objects *in* New York are 4.6-billion-year-old meteors and 10-billion-year-old stardust—actually, presolar grains in primitive chondrites—at the American Museum of Natural History. The oldest handcrafted object in Manhattan is considered to be the obelisk known as Cleopatra's Needle, dating from 1450 B.C. and installed in Central Park in 1881.)

The interlayered rock formations belowground are analogous to the intermixed neighborhoods on the surface. The granites are folded into tunnel walls exposed by monstrous rock-boring machines. The undulating formations are the bedrock that defines Manhattan's skyline. In midtown, bedrock is just below the asphalt. To build the World Trade Center, seventy-five feet of fill, glacial till, and muck had to be excavated until bedrock was reached. In between downtown and midtown, the bedrock surface dips into a deeper trough and the ground is relatively squishy, which means that a century or so ago, building a skyscraper there would have been too challenging for contemporary engineering. Today, while it may be prohibitively expensive, such construction is technologically possible. Good rocks, geologists like to say, make good foundations and good tunnels.

Underground Manhattan is laced with unseen, taken-for-granted tunnels, the latest of which is the East Side Access, 170 feet below Park Avenue. It stretches from the East Sixty-Third Street tunnel under the East River, which it shares with the subway from Queens, and terminates at East Thirty-Sixth Street, just below the Union League Club. (A Manhattan portion of the sixty-mile-long third water tunnel, which has been under construction for four decades and is scheduled for completion around 2020, opened in 2013; the Long Island Rail Road's direct East Side Access is now expected to start around 2020.)

Legally, landlords own the land beneath their property to the center of the earth, so tunnels require easements, which, in the case of government agencies, can be obtained through negotiation or by exercising the right of eminent domain. An advance team of geologists mines the excavations to verify topographical details of the original shoreline and underground water courses still derived from the pre-development 1865 map of Egbert Viele (a civil engineer and congressman), to adjust engineering specifications to the conditions that are discovered, and to leave a geological record for posterity. Finding amphibolite and similar rock formations migrating like baked taffy—one geologist likened the pattern to a Charleston Chew—in both Manhattan and Morocco provides evidence substantiating Alfred Wegener's once ridiculed theory of continental drift.

•2•

Mastodon Tusk

Before Skyscraper National Park

The first recorded discovery of mastodon remains in the city was in 1858, during the digging of the Baisley Pond reservoir in Queens, although unsubstantiated reports date earlier (including a large bone found ten feet below the basement of a house at Broadway near Franklin Street in 1840). In 1885, Elisha Howland, principal of a grammar school on West 128th Street, turned up with a fifteen-inch lower extremity of a mastodon tusk found buried in peat by ditch diggers near the Presbyterian church in Inwood in upper Manhattan.

That same year, excavations for the Harlem Ship Canal produced a three-foot-long mastodon or mammoth tusk sixteen feet below mean water level at the eastern end of Dyckman's Creek and the Harlem River. The dig was in a salt meadow under sod, silt, peat, sandy clay. The tusk was embedded with the butt end down. "It seems probable," wrote R. P. Whitfield of the American Museum of Natural History, "that the animal to which the tusk once belonged either died near the spot, or by some accidental injury had it broken from its socket near where it was found." By the time laborers on the canal unearthed a yard-long mastodon tusk in 1891, it must have seemed commonplace. The find merited only a paragraph in *The New York Times*.

Evidence that mastodons once roamed what is now Manhattan may still be found in an unusual form: honey locust trees, which survive on many streets. They are descendants of a species that paleoecologists say developed prickly spikes to deter mastodons from swallowing leaves and branches in one giant mouthful.

Eric Sanderson, an ecologist with the Wildlife Conservation Society in the Bronx, has written that as recently as four centuries ago, Manhattan had more separate ecological communities than Yellowstone, more native plant species than Yosemite, and more birds than the Great Smoky Mountains.

"If Mannahatta [as he calls it] existed today as it did then, it would be a national park," Sanderson says. "It would be the crowning glory of American National Parks."

Arrowhead

The Better to Shoot You

Humans ventured to New York at the end of the last ice age, and stone projectiles dated back about nine thousand years have been found near Port Mobil on Staten Island. Scattered prehistoric cultural artifacts—including hearths and crude spear points—found on a bluff overlooking Raritan Bay in Tottenville, Staten Island, attest to the presence of Paleo-Indians there at least eight thousand years ago. (The mastodons might have still been present.) The Iroquois arrived around the ninth century from the Appalachian region, and Algonquin tribes from Ontario and upstate New York. Their cultures, as Europeans would discover them, were largely developed by around the twelfth century. A New York State Historical Association study concluded that the Native Americans established "a complex and elaborate native economy that included hunting, gathering, manufacturing and farming." A mosaic of tribes, nations, languages, and political associations existed before what amounted to a colonial invasion.

Most local Indians were related to the Lenape—the "real people," by one definition. A plaque placed at the tip of Manhattan by the Smithsonian's National Museum of the American Indian describes the island paradise where they grew corn, beans, and squash: "Following the round of the seasons, the first people planted, hunted and fished in the spring. In the warmest season when the smell of wild flowers perfumed the air, they traveled for trade and adventure. . . . When the leaves changed color, the villagers gathered to harvest, hunt and collect food for the winter. During the cold moons and long nights they made objects for trade, repaired tools, told lesson stories and celebrated festivals."

A history edited by Hubert H. Bancroft early in the twentieth century recalled that the arriving Dutch were the beneficiaries of a war between the Five Nations of the Iroquois and the Algonquin, who were armed by the French in Canada. The Iroquois viewed the Dutch as a gun-toting potential ally. Bancroft's history concluded, "Though jealous by nature, and given to suspicion, the Indians exhibited none of these feelings towards the new-comers, whose numbers were too few even to protect themselves or to inflict injury on others. On the contrary, they courted their friendship, for through them they shrewdly calculated on being placed in a condition to cope with the foe, or to obtain that bloody triumph for which they thirsted."

The Staten Island site, known as Burial Ridge, was used as a graveyard thousands of years later by the Munsee and other branches of the Lenape, who witnessed Henry Hudson's approach in 1609. Evidence of later contact with Europeans was excavated, along with arrowheads made of bone, antler, stone, and metal.

Giovanni da Verrazano, an Italian sailing in 1524 for the king of France, reported that natives "clothed with the feathers of birds of various colors" approached his party "joyfully, uttering very great exclamations of admiration," and directed him to a safe mooring. Other Europeans followed, including Hudson, who disregarded the orders of his employer, the Dutch East India Company, and sailed west instead of seeking a northeast passage to India.

·4·

Crime Scene

Whodunit?

Typically, about half the homicides in New York City are solved within the first year. This one has remained a bit of a mystery for four centuries.

The victim was John Colman, an Englishman, accomplished sailor, and second mate aboard the *Half Moon* in 1609, as Henry Hudson explored the harbor and Upper Bay. It is the first recorded murder in New York.

The only existing account of the crime was gleaned from eyewitnesses by Robert Juet, aka Jouet, Hudson's first mate. After morning prayers on September 6, four crew members accompanied Colman in a sixteen-foot shallop on a reconnaissance mission from the *Half Moon*, anchored between Coney Island and Sandy Hook. They surveyed lands "as pleasant with grass and flowers and goodly trees as ever they had seen, and very sweet smells came from them." They sailed about six miles, possibly to Kill Van Kull, Newark Bay, or even farther north to Upper New York Bay, where they "saw an open sea."

Upon returning toward nightfall, "they were set upon by two canoes," one with twelve men and the other with fourteen. Colman was "slain in the fight," Juet wrote in his log, "with an arrow shot into his throat and two more hurt." (His chest may have been sheathed in armor, but he was struck in the neck by a stone arrowhead and bled to death.) The survivors drifted in the dark, their light having gone out in the rain (which also left them unable to ignite a small cannon, although they may have routed the marauders with musket fire). They returned to their ship by ten the next morning with the dead man, "whom we carried on land and buried and named the point"—probably some spot in Coney Island, Staten Island, Sandy Hook, or Keansburg, New Jersey (where a Colman's Point still exists)—"after his name."

Modern detectives say the perfunctory investigation, if not details of the murder itself, were suspect. The only account of the crime is secondhand, pieced to-

gether from a few witnesses among a largely Dutch crew, some of whom might have harbored a grudge against the Englishman. (Colman, in a letter to his wife, contemptuously wrote of the Dutch men: "Looking at their fat bellies, I fear they think more highly of eating than of sailing.")

Colman had served Hudson as a trusted boatswain on an earlier voyage, but Juet was described by Hudson himself as mean-tempered, and later led a mutiny against the captain. Colman's body was hastily buried and has never been found. The arrow was recovered but vanished. The chief suspects were singled out because of racial profiling but were never questioned. No one was ever prosecuted. Just two days after the murder, Juet recounted, natives boarded the *Half Moon* to trade while the crew kept a careful watch to "see if they would show any sign of the death of our man, which they did not" (suggesting that they were either innocent or duplicitous or that the killers had come from a different tribe).

The murder is memorialized in a mural in the Hudson County Courthouse in Jersey City and in a poem by Thomas Frost that hinted at Colman's disdain for the crew:

> *"What! are ye cravens?" Colman said;*
> *For each had shipped his oar.*
> *He waved the flag: "For Netherland,*
> *Pull for yon jutting shore!"*
> *Then prone he fell within the boat,*
> *A flinthead arrow through his throat!*

·5·

Birth Certificate

The Greatest Sale on Earth

It is New York's birth certificate, the closest history comes to recording the Indians' "sale" of Manhattan island for twenty-four dollars to the Dutch, who first settled on Governors Island and then uprooted themselves again to hop another half mile to what would become Lower Manhattan.

The document is known as the "Schaghenbrief," a letter from Pieter Schaghen, a Dutch parliamentary representative of the West India Company, to his "High and Mighty Lords" in the Haarlemmerstraat in Amsterdam. Dated November 5, 1626, the letter informs the Dutch Parliament of recent events related by the crew of the ship *Arms of Amsterdam*, which left the New World ("It sailed from New Netherland out of the River Mauritius") on September 23, 1626, and arrived in Amsterdam on November 4.

Schaghen dutifully reports that some children were born, that summer grains were sown and reaped, and he catalogs the ship's cargo, including 7,246 beaver skins, 178½ otter skins, 48 mink skins, 36 lynx skins, 33 minks, 34 muskrat skins, and oak timbers and nutwood and samples of summer grains. In between, he notes incidentally that the settlers "have purchased the Island Manhattes from the Indians for the value of 60 guilders"—signaling the beginning of European exploitation.

'SRYKS
ARCHIEF.

7 november 1626

Hooghe Moghende Heeren

Hier is gisteren t'schip t'wapen van Amsterdam
aengekomen den is de 23 septm. uyt Nieue Nederlant gezeylt uyt de Riuier Mauritius. rapporteren
dat ons volck daer kloec is in vreddige Leuen
haere vrouwen hebben oic kinderen aldaer gebaert
hebben t'eylant Manhattes van de wilde gekocht, voor
de waerde van 60. gul. is groot 11000 margen.
hebbende alle koren gesaeyt medio maey, ende gaue
augusto gemaeyt. Daer van zyndende munsterkens
van zomerkoren, als taruwe, Rogge, garst, haber
boeckweyt, kanariezaet, boontjens en vlas.

Het Cargasoen van t'sz schip is

7246 Bever vellen
178½ Otter vellen
675. Otter vellen
48. Mincke vellen
36. Catloss vellen
33 Minckes
34 Ratte Vellekens.

Veel eycken Balcken, en Noten hout.

Hier mede
Hooghe Moghende heeren, zyt de Almoghende
in genade bevolen.

In Amsterdam den 5e novem a[o] 1626.

Uwe Hoo: Moo: Dienstwillighe

P Schaghen

A curator at the Rijksmuseum in Amsterdam, Martine Gosselink, described the Schaghenbrief as "not only evidence of the agreement concluded between the local population and the Dutch in 1626, but also of the first children born to the pioneers in the Dutch colony."

No actual deed or documentation has been found directly linking Peter Minuit, the director of the colony, to the sale, which was to have taken place that May. Nor does any document specify what the Indians received that was worth sixty guilders (the same price the Dutch would pay later that year, in tools, beads, and other goods, for Staten Island and, much later, famously estimated at twenty-four dollars in goods). The settlers figured the island's size at about 22,000 acres, which would be roughly 34 square miles. (Manhattan today, grown by landfill, is 23 square miles, so the Dutch may have overestimated—and perhaps overpaid—or were including additional territory; that would be cheaper per acre than the Louisiana Purchase, or the price the U.S. paid Russia for Alaska.) By comparison, though, the ship's cargo of nearly 8,000 animal skins was worth about 45,000 guilders.

Fortune magazine has dubbed this "the best business deal ever made." (The market value of Manhattan real estate today is well over $320 billion.) Still, while the Dutch settlers were instructed to negotiate a sale rather than seize the land, the Indians were largely unfamiliar with European concepts of property ownership. Moreover, some Indians were migratory, so their presence in Manhattan in the summer of 1626 did not necessarily mean they lived there full-time or "owned" it.

Schaghen reported that "our people are in good spirit and live in peace." Peace did not last for long. In 1640, the Dutch launched an unprovoked attack on the Indians. The Indians never recovered.

•6•

Flushing Remonstrance

"In God We Trust"

New Amsterdammers didn't always get along with each other, either. On December 27, 1657, residents of the town of Flushing, in what became Queens, formally challenged the fiat by New Amsterdam's director-general Peter Stuyvesant against practicing Quakers and his public torture of a convert to Quakerism. New Amsterdam had earned a reputation for tolerance toward ethnic, racial, and religious diversity, but there were limits. The settlers' response to Stuyvesant, an orthodox Calvinist, became known as the Flushing Remonstrance. It was a vital antecedent of the provision in the Bill of Rights for freedom of religion, which would be forged in the following century in New York.

Their petition is considered especially noteworthy for two reasons: It rebuffed, respectfully, a demonstrably intolerant public official who was not receptive to criticism of any sort; and unlike so many other divisions in New Amsterdam, it was not motivated by personal animus. It was, without equivocation, a matter of principle.

"If any of these said persons come in love unto us," the Flushing residents wrote, referring to the Quakers, "we cannot in conscience lay violent hands upon them, but give them free egress and regress unto our town." In other words, Quak-

William Thorne signior

The marke of M William Thorne Junr

Edward Tarte +   The marke off M

John Stover   The marke of P
Nathaniel [mark]   Philip
Beniamin Hubbard

The marke ✗ of William Pidgion

The marke of Sudeyes Slade
Eliab Doughtie
Antonie Feild
Richard Horton
Edward Griffind
Nathaniell Tue
Robert Feild senior
~~Richard Harvie~~

Robert Feild Junior
Nicholas Parsell
Michaell Milur
~~Beniamin Hubbard~~

Henry Townsend
George Cwright
John Soard
Henry Fanttee
Edward Heart
~~John Haskins~~
Townsend
Harrington

ers who came in peace would not be harmed. The gist of the remonstrance was straightforward; while Stuyvesant claimed that Quakers were spiritual seducers, New Amsterdammers were supposed to respect all the faithful:

"We are bound by the law to do good unto all men, especially to those of the household of faith. . . . And though for the present we seem to be unsensible for the law and the Law giver, yet when death and the Law assault us, if we have our advocate to seek, who shall plead for us in this case of conscience betwixt God and our own souls; the powers of this world can neither attach us, neither excuse us, for if God justify who can condemn and if God condemn there is none can justify. . . . The law of love, peace and liberty in the states extending to Jews, Turks and Egyptians, as they are considered sons of Adam, which is the glory of the outward state of Holland, so love, peace and liberty, extending to all in Christ Jesus, condemns hatred, war and bondage."

The Flushing townsfolk made clear they were not being rebellious against New Netherland or the Dutch Reformed Church; just the opposite. They wrote that their position was "according to the patent and charter of our Towne, given unto us in the name of the States General, which we are not willing to infringe, and violate." That patent—issued in 1645, when most Flushing residents were English— granted them the right "to have and enjoy the liberty of conscience, according to the custom and the manner of Holland, without molestation or disturbance."

Governor Stuyvesant disagreed. He jailed the town clerk, then banished him from New Netherland. The town government was replaced with Stuyvesant's acolytes. Finally, after Stuyvesant was rebuked by the Dutch West India Company directors for mistreatment of Jews and just before he was dethroned by the British, they warned him to refrain from further religious persecution.

Built in 1694 by John Bowne and other early Quakers, the Old Quaker Meeting House still stands in Flushing, a simple rectangular building framed by oak timbers and topped by a steep-hipped roof modeled on medieval Holland. It is said to be the oldest house of worship in New York.

·7·

Dictionary

A Colonial Rosetta Stone

Disgusted with Peter Stuyvesant's capricious rule since 1647 and egged on even by Stuyvesant's own son, New Amsterdam's merchants and civic leaders surrendered to a four-warship English naval squadron in 1664, effectively ending four decades of Dutch rule. The victorious Colonel Richard Nicholls claimed the settlement for the duke of York, who had sponsored the mission in the midst of yet another English naval war with the Dutch.

The twenty-three-point articles of capitulation could barely have been more gracious. The goal of the agreement was continuity, not subjugation. Why tinker with a good thing? Religious and other freedoms would be tolerated. The agreement permitted ongoing immigration from the Netherlands and maintenance of property and goods, including arms; declared that "all differences of contracts and bargains made before this day by any in this country shall be determined according to the manner of the Dutch"; and perhaps most felicitously, allowed that "all public Houses shall continue for the uses, which now they are for."

As the duke's secretary said of the Dutch, "Their trade is their god," and the town's merchants envisioned a uniquely diverse and tolerant—or indifferent—society that would be New Amsterdam's most enduring legacy, regardless of which foreign power claimed control. (Ironically, while the duke of York's elevation as king would transform New York into a crown colony, when he produced a Catholic heir, he was deposed in the Glorious Revolution of 1688—by an invading army from the Netherlands led by his Protestant son-in-law and nephew, William III of Orange.)

Language difficulties divided the population (about half of it Dutch at the time) and got in the way of the British laissez-faire approach to governing. Innovations like the jury system were particularly problematic. The problem was solved

THE

English and *Low-Dutch*

SCHOOL-MASTER.

CONTAINING

Alphabetical Tables of the most Common Words in *English* and *Dutch*. With certain Rules and Directions whereby the *Low-Dutch* Inhabitants of *North-America* may (in a short time) learn to Spell, Read, Understand and Speak proper *English*. And by the help whereof the *English* may also learn to Spell, Read, Understand and Write Low-Dutch.

By *FRANCIS HARRISON*,

School-Master, in *Somerset-County*, in *New-Jersey*, *America*.

NEW-YORK:

Printed and Sold by *W. Bradford*. 1730.

DE

Engelsche en *Nederduytsche*

SCHOOL - MEESTER.

BEHELSENDE

Verschydene Tafelen, na de order van *A, B,* in gericht van de gemeenste Woorden, in 't *Engels* en *Duytsch*. Met eenige Regels en Onderwysingen, waardoor de *Nederduytsche* Inwoonders van *Nort America* in korten tyt de *Engelsche* Taal mogen leeren *Spellen, Leesen, Verstaan* en *Spreeken*. Ende de *Engelsche* in 's gelyks mogen leeren *Spellen, Leesen, Verstaan* en *Schryven*, in de *Nederduytsche* Taal.

Opgestelt door *FRANCIS HARRISON*, School-Meester, in *Somerset-County*, in *Nieuw-Jersy*, in *America*.

NIEUW-JORK:

Gedrukt en te Koop by *W. Bradfordt*. 1730.

by an English–Low Dutch dictionary published by a New Jersey schoolmaster. Except for a brief Dutch restoration nine years later, the English would rule for over a century. Their language would, more or less, prevail. Among the enduring linguistic traditions of the Dutch is that we still call little chunks of dough "cookies," instead of the British "biscuits". Other words such as "coleslaw," "waffle," "doughnut," "stoop," and "Yankee" endured.

So did one living legacy of the Dutch hegemony and of Peter Stuyvesant: a pear tree that he planted upon his arrival in New Amsterdam on his farm, which encompassed what is now the East Village. The tree stood on what would become the corner of Third Avenue and East Thirteenth Street for over two centuries, until it was felled in 1867, when two horse carts collided nearby and one careered into the ancient trunk. A cross-section is preserved at the New-York Historical Society. Except for descendants of a few Dutch families, Stuyvesant's pear tree appeared to be the last direct living floral connection to New York's Dutch heritage. In the twenty-first century, Bronxites would discover a faunal link.

•8•

Beaver

Two Tails of a City

Not many cities have animals in their official seals. New York has two. Given their significance, it's none too many.

The relevance of the year on the seal—1625—is arguable, but not the symbolism of the two beavers that flank the blades of a windmill, signifying New Amsterdam's Dutch heritage and fur-trading foundation, and complemented by flour barrels, which reflect the monopoly on exports that boosted New York's economy. The union—however tenuous at times—between settlers and Indians is represented by Dexter, a uniformed sailor, holding a plummet with a cross-staff (used in navigation) above his shoulder, and Sinister, a nearly naked Lenape, who is clutching a bow.

The date of the founding of New York on the city seal had been 1664 for over half a century. That was the date when the Dutch surrendered the city to the British. Nobody complained much about the date until 1974, when Paul O'Dwyer, the Irish-born and Anglophobic president of the City Council, decided to strip the British of the distinction of having founded the city and bestow it instead on the Dutch.

But how to define "founded"? The City Council, familiar in those days with

obliterating the past by changing street names to honor more contemporary wor-
thies, was suddenly thrust into a debate of, well, historic proportions. Some schol-
ars persuaded O'Dwyer that if the pretext was to honor the Dutch contribution,
1624—the date he wanted—might be difficult to justify. The first settlers who ar-

rived on Governors Island in 1624 in the Dutch West India Company ship *Nieuw Amsterdam* were mostly Walloons from Belgium who had sought asylum in the Netherlands from religious persecution during the Spanish Inquisition. Also, many moved on to Albany. So O'Dwyer and the Council opted for 1625, he sniffed, because that was when New Amsterdam was "designated by the Dutch West India Company as the seat of government for all lands held by the Netherlands in this continent," while 1664 signified only "the year in which the city leaders took 'the oath of allegiance to England.'" That same day in 1975 when Mayor Abraham D. Beame approved the date-change bill, he also signed legislation to change the Anglophilic name of the borough of Richmond to Staten Island (it remains Richmond County).

The beavers on the city seal survived the transition (no animal rights protesters weighed in), and they have since thrived. In 2007, a beaver nicknamed José, reflecting the borough's changing demographics, was spotted building a lodge in the Bronx River adjacent to the Bronx Zoo. Scientists described it as the first confirmed sighting in about two centuries in the environmentally revived river. José was joined a few years later by Justin Beaver.

·9·

Oyster

The Bivalve Bonanza

To anyone who is familiar with New Yorkers," Mark Kurlansky wrote in *The Big Oyster,* "it should not be surprising to learn that they were once famous for eating their food live." If New Yorkers are what they eat, then beginning in the seventeenth century, no food epitomized them and their city more than the oyster. It was New York's culinary obsession, an enduring, profitable, and edible version of the tulipmania that captivated the Dutch.

"He was a bold man that first ate an oyster," Jonathan Swift famously wrote. That first bold man dates to prehistoric times. Henry Hudson was greeted by natives who "brought great store of very good oysters aboard," Joannes DeLaet, a geographer whose map was the first to mention Manhattan, reported in 1625. The Dutch originally named Liberty and Ellis islands Great and Little Oyster, although they were initially chagrined that the local variety, which grew to nine inches and even longer in the brackish harbor, did not produce pearls. New Yorkers embraced them anyway (although city fathers drew the line at the burning of oyster shells to produce lime and refused a permit in 1810 for an oyster stand directly in front of the new City Hall).

By the nineteenth century, New York Harbor had become the largest source of oysters in the world. They were baked into oyster pie, served raw (later popularized by Delmonico's), and hawked by street vendors. Oysters were cheap; they were eaten pickled, stewed, roasted, fried, and scalloped; in soups, patties, and puddings; for breakfast, lunch, and dinner. If a customer on the so-called Canal Street plan (all you can eat for six cents) consumed too many, Kurlansky wrote, the management would give him an oyster with its shell loosely open "in the hopes that after a few minutes, the avaricious client would be eating nothing for several days."

Oyster shells were so ubiquitous that they were eventually used to pave Pearl Street (and gave it its name) and to supply lime for the mortar for Trinity Church. Shell middens or mounds were found all over Manhattan, rare surviving evidence of Native American civilizations. Their popularity gave rise to restaurants and provided thousands of skilled jobs for cultivators, but the beds would become exhausted by rising demand. Importation of foreign species produced disease, and sewage and silt did in the rest.

New beds in the harbor have been seeded, although they may not be safe to harvest for decades. Still, the Oyster Bar, Grand Central Terminal's first tenant when it opened in 1913, still serves five million bivalve mollusks a year. "Enjoy the oysters," visitors to New York were typically advised. They still can.

·10·

Guidebook

The Lure of Going West

John L. O'Sullivan's 1845 column in the *New York Morning News* popularized Americans' mission of "manifest destiny." In 1865, Horace Greeley's *New-York Tribune* urged his young male readers to "Go West" (particularly if given the opportunity to go to Washington, D.C., instead). Daniel Denton, the son of the first Presbyterian minister in America and himself later the county clerk of Queens, had both of them beat by two centuries. His 1670 promotional tract, intended primarily for English-speaking audiences, extolled the virtues of free land and unlimited future in New York and the opportunity to expand that opportunity far beyond its borders.

His *A Brief Description of New-York: Formerly Called New Netherland* delivered on its title. It was only about twenty-five pages. His romanticized Baedeker was among the first of thousands of guidebooks to the city and a swipe at the Dutch, who had just relinquished control to the duke of York.

Much like Greeley, Denton suggested his readers "grow up with the country" in a new world that held the prospect of good fortune. Denton largely discounted potential adversity, particularly the hostility of Native Americans toward encroaching settlers. Yet in an apparent contradiction, he sanguinely suggested that the

A
Brief Description
OF
NEW-YORK:
Formerly Called
New-Netherlands.
With the Places thereunto Adjoyning.

Together with the

Manner of its Scituation, Fertility of the Soyle,
Healthfulness of the Climate, and the
Commodities thence produced.

ALSO

Some Directions and Advice to such as shall go
thither: An Account of what Commodities they shall
take with them; The Profit and Pleasure that
may accrew to them thereby.

LIKEWISE

A Brief RELATION of the Customs of the
Indians there.

10

By *DANIEL DENTON.*

LONDON,
Printed for *John Hancock*, at the first Shop in *Popes-Head-Al'ey* in
Cornhill at the three Bibles, and *William Bradley* at the three Bibles

British would prove more effective at controlling the Indian population than the Dutch had been.

Writing from London, where, presumably, he could be more dispassionate after several decades in the New World, Denton expressed optimism that English settlers would be fruitful because "a Divine Hand makes way for them by removing or cutting off the Indians, either by wars one with the other, or by some raging mortal disease."

Denton was not merely in the advance guard of New York chauvinists. He was in the forefront of another local tradition: opportunism. As a land speculator, he might well have stood to benefit from any influx of settlers lured by his pamphlet, which extolled the virtues of "Minahatans," Long Island and Staten Island and the potential that awaited on both banks of the river of empire that Henry Hudson had navigated only six decades before.

The climate was healthful. The settlers were content. The harbor was naturally defensible (though Denton presciently warned against the roiling currents of Hell Gate). He wistfully alluded to Dutch claims of gold and silver deposits but also envisioned the garment center ("they would in a little time live without the help of any other country for their clothing").

Without specifying that England be depopulated of its less fortunate, he repeatedly invoked New York's egalitarianism ("where a wagon or cart gives as good content as a coach") and its abundance of land ("How many poor people in the world would think themselves happy, had they an acre or two of land, whilst here is hundreds, nay thousands of acres," and here those "which fortune hath frown'd upon in England" could thrive). In short, he said, "if there be any terrestrial Canaan, 'tis surely here."

Numb. XVII.

THE
New-York Weekly JOURNAL.

Containing the freſheſt Advices, Foreign, and Domeſtick.

MUNDAY February 25, 1733.

Mr. Zenger;

As Libeling ſeems at Preſent the Topick that is canvaſſed both at Court and among the People, I muſt beg you will inſert in your weekly Journal; the following Sentiments of CATO, upon that Subject, and you'll oblige

Your humble Servant, &c,

A Lible is not the leſs a Libel for being true, this may ſeem a Contradiction; but it is neither one in Law, or in common Senſe. There are ſome Truths not fit to be told; where, for Example, the Diſcovery of a ſmall Fault may do miſchief; or where the Diſcovery of a great Fault can do no good, there ought to be no diſcovery at all, and to make Faults where there are none is ſtill worſe.

But this Doctrine only holds true as to private and perſonal failings; and it is quite otherwiſe when the Crimes of Men come to Affect the Publick. Nothing ought to be ſo dear to us as our Country, and nothing ought to come in Competition with its Intereſts. Every crime againſt the publick, is a great crime, tho' there be ſome greater than others. Ignorance and Folly may be pleaded in Alleviation of private Offences; but when they come to be publick Offences, they looſe all Benefit of ſuch a Plea; we are then no longer to conſider, to what Cauſes they are owing, but what Evils they may produce, and here we ſhall readily find, that Folly has overturned States, and private Intereſt been the parent of publick Confuſion.

The expoſing therefore of publick Wickedneſs, as it is a Duty which every Man owes to Truth and his Country, can never be a Libel in the Nature of Things; and they who call it ſo, make themſelves no Complement; he who is affronted at the reading of the Ten Commandments would make the Decalogue a Libel, if he durſt, but he Tempts us at the ſame Time to form a Judgment of his Life and Morals, not at all to his Advantage: Whoever calls publick and neceſſary Truths Libels, does appriſe us of his own Character, and Arms us with Caution againſt his Deſigns.

I have long thought, that the World are very much miſtaken in their Idea and Diſtinction of Libels, it has been hitherto generally underſtood, that there was no other Libels but thoſe againſt Magiſtrates and thoſe againſt private Men. Now to me there ſeems to be a Third ſort of Libels, full as Deſtructive as any of the former can probably be, I mean Libels againſt the People. It was otherwiſe at Athens and Rome, where the particular Men, and even great Men, were often treated with much Freedom and Severity; when they deſerved it; yet the People, the body of the People, were ſpoken of with the utmoſt Regard and Reverence. *The Sacred Priviledge of the People, the Inviolable Majeſty of the People, the awful Authority of the People, and the unappealable Judgment of the People,* were phraſes Common in theſe wiſe, great and free Cities.

Some will tell us, this is ſetting up the Mob for Stateſmen, and for the cenſurers of States. The word Mob does not at all move me, on this Occaſion, nor weaken the Ground I go upon, it is certain that the whole People, who are the publick, are the beſt Judges, whether Things go ill or well, with the publick. It is true they can't all of them ſee diſtant Dangers, nor watch the Motions, nor gueſs the deſigns of neighbouring States: But every

Coble

·11·
Newspaper

The Prints of the City

Not everyone was as content under British rule as Daniel Denton imagined. They were particularly peeved by the capriciousness of William Cosby, the Irish-born scion of an aristocratic British family who became the British royal governor of New York in 1732. He was litigious, unpopular, neglectful of his official duties, guilty of gross political manipulation, and overly generous with official favors to his loyal subjects. Most enduringly, Cosby was on the losing end of a legal decision that indelibly established freedom of the press in New York.

The vehicle for that freedom was the *New-York Weekly Journal,* an anti-royalist newspaper published by John Peter Zenger, a German immigrant, and funded by allies of Lewis Morris, the former State Supreme Court chief justice whom Cosby had fired for ruling against him in a salary dispute.

The dispute gave rise to the Popular Party, and subsequent articles in the *Journal,* founded specifically to oppose Cosby, regularly castigated the governor for abuse of power. The writers were anonymous, including James Alexander, a Popular Party founder, to whom is attributed an editorial that concluded: "No nation ancient or modern has ever lost the liberty of freely speaking, writing or publishing their sentiments, but forthwith lost their liberty in general and became slaves."

The only name publicly associated with the weekly was that of its printer, Zenger. Two grand juries refused to charge Zenger with seditious libel, but the governor's Provincial Council ordered his arrest on November 17, 1734, almost a year to the day since the paper debuted. He was jailed in a third-floor cell at City Hall for over eight months. The paper kept publishing, thanks to his wife, Anna, and friends from the Popular Party.

After his own lawyers were disbarred by a Cosby ally, Andrew Hamilton of Philadelphia was recruited for the defense (legend has it that Hamilton's reputation as a stickler and highly regarded litigator gave rise to the term "Philadelphia lawyer"). The trial began August 4, 1735, on the main floor of City Hall, now the site of Federal Hall National Memorial on Wall Street. The prosecutor accused Zenger of "wickedly and maliciously" seeking to "traduce, scandalize and vilify" the governor, adding ominously: "Libeling has always been discouraged as a thing that tends to create differences among men, ill blood among the people, and often-times great bloodshed between the party libeling and the party libeled."

Hamilton, contrary to English law, invoked the truth as a defense. He delivered a stem-winding closing argument to the jury: "It is not the cause of one poor printer, nor of New York alone, which you are now trying. No! It may in its conse-quence affect every free man that lives under a British government on the main of America. It is the best cause. It is the cause of liberty."

A little over a half century later, Congress passed the Bill of Rights in the same downtown building where Zenger was tried and acquitted. "The trial of Zenger in 1735," wrote Gouverneur Morris, a drafter of the Constitution, "was the germ of American freedom, the morning star of that liberty which subsequently revolution-ized America."

·12·

Horse's Tail

A Royal Ending

Araucous public rendition of the Declaration of Independence on July 9, 1776, inspired New Yorkers to converge on Bowling Green, the city's first public park, where they hacked off the crown-shaped finials on a wrought-iron fence (the fence remains there today) and toppled and beheaded the gilded equestrian statue of King George III.

A nineteen-inch remnant of the tail wound up in the New-York Historical Society. The horse's head was somehow spirited away by Tories and smuggled to England, where it was last seen at, of all places, the home of Lord Charles Townshend. It was Townshend, as the chancellor of the exchequer, who inspired other hated taxes on the American colonies in 1767, following the repeal of the Stamp Act. Repeal prompted grateful New Yorkers to commission (from Joseph Wilton in London) the four-thousand-pound statue of George III in Roman garb "to perpetuate to the latest posterity, the deep sense this colony has of the eminent and singular blessings received from him during his most auspicious reign." The statue was dedicated with a thirty-two-gun salute on April 26, 1770, from adjacent Fort George, the British redoubt.

The colonists' gratitude was short-lived. An anti-desecration statute was im-

posed to discourage wanton vandalism. (George Washington objected to his sol-diers' involvement in the mob assault on the statue in 1776, suggesting the military leave any such displays of protest to "the proper authorities.") Much of the lead statue was melted to make musket balls or bullets for the Continental Army—42,088 of them in a Litchfield, Connecticut, foundry belonging to General Oliver Wolcott, a member of the Continental Congress and signer of the Declaration. "One wit predicted," the historian Ron Chernow wrote, "that the king's soldiers 'will probably have melted majesty fired at them.'"

By some measures, the toppling of the king's statue was the first official act of rebellion after independence was declared. It assumed mythic proportions. In sub-sequent paintings (by Johannes Adam Simon Oertel) and engravings (by John C. McRae), the protesters included women, children, African-Americans, and Native Americans in subsidiary roles.

While Washington was irked by the mob rule against the king, he apparently had no such compunctions about a subsequent plot, hatched by one of his colo-nels, to kidnap Prince William, the heir to the throne, who was stationed in New York. The plot was abandoned after the British got wind of it and doubled the prince's guards.

After the colonies were lost and he succeeded his father as king, William, fet-ing the American minister to London, declared that he regretted not having "been born a free, independent American, so much did he respect that nation, which had given birth to Washington, the greatest man that ever lived."

· 13 ·

Fire Pail

Saving St. Paul's

Just one week after the British invaded Manhattan in September 1776, a suspicious fire destroyed as much as a quarter of the city, hundreds of the estimated four thousand buildings. A hastily organized bucket brigade drawing water from the Hudson River saved St. Paul's Chapel, which had opened in 1766 and remains Manhattan's oldest and only existing prerevolutionary public building in continuous use.

The fire was said to have broken out shortly after midnight at the Fighting Cocks Tavern near Whitehall Slip. It quickly consumed Trinity Church, but the Reverend Charles Inglis, Trinity's assistant minister, rallied men, women, and children to soak the roof of St. Paul's, about a third of a mile away. The fire not only inflicted immediate hardship but would exacerbate the misery inflicted by the prolonged British occupation of New York. Survivors pitched canvas tents on the charred ruins. Loyalists flooded into the city, and both public and private buildings were appropriated to house them and billet British troops.

Patriots suspected the British of setting the blaze; the British, meanwhile, suspected American arsonists, and with good reason. George Washington disclaimed any advance knowledge of the fire but wrote his cousin: "Providence—or some good honest Fellow, has done more for us than we were disposed to do for ourselves." As a result of their suspicions, the British imposed martial law for the duration of their seven-year occupation. (Perhaps not coincidentally, on that very day, Nathan Hale was arrested in Queens as an American spy.) Their cruel treatment of captured American soldiers consigned to filthy prison ships off Brooklyn may have been another consequence of the suspicion and animosity that the fire created in the occupied city.

St. Paul's miraculous survival in the Great Fire was mirrored on September 11, 2001, when the World Trade Center collapsed. Standing in the shadow of the Twin Towers, the church was unharmed. Not a single window was broken. For months, the chapel served as a sanctuary for police, firemen, construction workers, and volunteers at the site. The iron gates of the chapel were festooned with photographs of the missing, teddy bears, flowers, and other tributes.

About a decade later, Omayra Rivera, St. Paul's thirty-seven-year-old program director, maneuvered herself behind the 1804 pipe organ and made her way to the steeple after hearing maintenance workers discussing artifacts they discovered there. She found what may have been evidence of the chapel's original miracle: a three-gallon leather bucket marked "St. Paul's, 1768," the year when tougher fire regulations took effect.

·14·

Stone Slab

Washington Stepped Here

You could say with great assurance that George Washington stepped here, "here" being the second-floor balcony of what is now the Federal Hall National Memorial at 26 Wall Street. Washington was inaugurated as the first president there on April 30, 1789, after Peter L'Enfant renovated New York's old City Hall into the nation's first Capitol.

In keeping with the city's early commitment to recycling, the century-old building was razed in 1812 and sold for $450 in scrap after Congress decamped first for Philadelphia and then for the swampy banks of the Potomac. (The first City Hall had stood at 71 Pearl Street and was sold in 1699.) Among the few relics salvaged from the second City Hall was a brownstone slab, nine feet by four feet, on which Washington stood during the ceremony. (It is on display at Federal Hall, along with a portion of the original balcony railing and the Bible with which he took the oath of office.)

The inauguration marked Washington's triumphal return to New York. When the city was the capital under the Articles of Confederation (from 1785 to 1788), he dubbed New York "the Seat of the Empire"—which is believed to be the source of its nickname, the Empire State.

The city he returned to as president was poised for imperial promise. "One of the great advantages of the Constitution over the Articles of Confederation," Harvard Professor Edward L. Glaeser wrote, "is that the Constitution significantly reduced the barriers to interstate trade. As these barriers fell, the possibility for interstate trade rose and the advantage of a location near the center of the colonies increased." That augured well for the proposed Potomac site that Washington favored. After 1790, New York would no longer be the capital city, the role it played under the Constitution from March 4, 1789 through December 5, 1790. Instead, it would become the city of capital. Historians still debate whether Alexander Hamilton shortchanged the city when he agreed to relocate the capital in the South in exchange for federal assumption of the states' Revolutionary War debt. Colum-

bia's Kenneth T. Jackson, for one, doesn't think so. "New York became the mercantile and financial capital first of the nation and then the world," he said, "and maybe its excitement and vitality derive from the fact that it lacks the boring buildings and boring people who are part of the permanent bureaucracy."

James Madison and Thomas Jefferson wanted a Southern capital. Hamilton wanted the new federal government to assume the debts of the states, incurred mostly in the North. After Jefferson ran into Hamilton at Washington's house on Cherry Street in Lower Manhattan, the three Founding Fathers agreed to meet for dinner at Jefferson's home at 57 Maiden Lane. There, they compromised. In July 1790, the Residence Act was passed, followed by the Assumption Act, and the capital decamped for a Southern, racially segregated city after an interim stay in Philadelphia. "When all is done," Abigail Adams wrote prophetically, "it will not be Broadway."

·15·

Burial Beads

Free at Last

While white men won their rights, other Americans remained, at best, second-class citizens. Bittersweet nostalgia for the immigrant experience was rarely generated among enslaved blacks, most of whose ancestors arrived in the Americas as slaves. Slavery was originally practiced by the Dutch West India Company by custom, not law. "It was the company's labor force of enslaved Africans," wrote Edna Greene Medford, a history professor at Howard University, "who carved some semblance of a civilization out of the wilderness."

Slavery is older than New York itself. It began in 1626, when the Dutch West India Company imported eleven African slaves. They were partially freed from servitude to the company in 1644, in what was billed as America's first emancipation proclamation.

After the British seized the settlement, blacks accounted for about 700 of New York's 5,000 residents. More than 4 in 10 New York households were slaveholders. Simmering racial tension exploded in 1741 in a purported plot to burn the city. Scores were arrested. Leslie Harris, a professor at Emory University, wrote that "no part of the colonial North relied more heavily on slavery than Manhattan. By the end of the 17th century, New York City had a larger black population than any other North American city. The ratio of slaves to whites in the total population was comparable to that in Maryland and Virginia at the time. In the 18th century, New York City was second only to Charleston and New Orleans in the number of slaves it held." While New York became a locus of abolitionism, "Northern slavery was largely obliterated from memory because it didn't serve the North's version of the Civil War," Mac Griswold wrote in *The Manor*.

From as early as 1627 to the end of the eighteenth century, as many as fifteen thousand free and enslaved blacks were buried in a 6.6-acre racially segregated site north of City Hall outside the original town limits. The site was unearthed in 1991, during the early stages of construction of a federal courthouse downtown. Archaeologists found the remains of a middle-aged woman buried with hundreds of beads around her waist, suggesting, according to Steven Laise, the National Park Service's chief of cultural resources for Manhattan sites, that she was accorded "considerable honor and prominence." Others showed symptoms of malnutrition and hard labor.

In 1785, after the Revolution, New Yorkers founded a Manumission Society.

Its agenda: the gradual abolition of slavery and support for free blacks. In 1799 the state declared that children born to slaves were required to be indentured servants until they were young adults. Slaves were finally freed as of July 4, 1827 (the 1840 census listed none, for the first time), although, Harris wrote, "white New Yorkers attempted to define and contain the free black community based on their assumptions that the experience of slavery had degraded blacks." Moreover, until the Civil War, Southern planters would be joined by their enslaved retinue when they visited their bankers and buyers in the city.

· 16 ·

Buttonwood Agreement

Their Word Was Their Bond

Probably no tree played a bigger role in New York history than a lone buttonwood that stood on the north side of Wall Street at number 68, between William and Pearl. Twenty-four merchants and brokers convened there on May 17, 1792, and signed an agreement that would become the framework for what emerged in 1817 as the New York Stock & Exchange Board and in 1863 as the New York Stock Exchange. On a single sheet of paper that became known as the Buttonwood Agreement, the brokers agreed to charge commissions of no less than one quarter of a percentage point and to "give preference to each other in our negotiations."

The tree lasted under a century—it was toppled by a storm on June 14, 1865—but the agreement has endured in spirit through mergers and unimaginable expansion for well over two centuries. (The historic tree was an American sycamore with mottled bark, the name buttonwood survives largely as a financial markets column in *The Economist*.)

The signers—a relatively diverse group that included five Jewish brokers—are immortalized in downtown street names, among them Barclay and Bleecker. No current members of the Exchange are direct descendants of the signers. They would meet at the Merchant's Coffee House and later convene at the Tontine, a

We the Subscribers, Brokers for the Purchase and Sale of Public Stock, do hereby solemnly promise and pledge ourselves to each other, that we will not buy or sell from this day for any person whatsoever, any kind of Public Stock, at a less rate than one quarter per Cent Commission on the Specie value of and that we will give a preference to each other in our Negotiations. In Testimony whereof we have set our hands this 17th day of May at New York. 1792.

Leond. Bleecker

Hugh Smith

Armstrong Barnewall

Sam March

Bernd Hart

Alexr. Zuntz

Andrew D. Barclay

Sutton & Hardy

Benjan. Seixas

John Henry

John A. Hardenbrook

Anml. Barber

Benn. Wistot

Jno. Ferrers

coffeehouse at 82 Wall, on the northwest corner of Water Street, where they would meet regularly until they outgrew the space in 1817. Brokers met in a trading room on the three-story building's second floor, but the Tontine also became the haunt of power brokers; traders who bought and sold slaves at the Meal Market across the street; and ship captains who registered their cargo of sugar, coffee, tea, molasses, cotton, and human beings. The Tontine was a nest of gossip, gambling, after-hours trading, and political intrigue—probably where the power lunch was born. According to one eyewitness, it was "filled with underwriters, brokers, merchants, traders, and politicians; selling, purchasing, trafficking, or insuring; some reading, others eagerly inquiring the news. Everything was in motion; all was life, bustle and activity."

The Stock Exchange's main building, which opened in 1903 and is a neoclassic national historic landmark, is located at 18 Broad Street, the trading floor at 11 Wall. The six columns of the main building support a pediment adorned by the sculpture *Integrity Protecting the Works of Man.* On September 16, 1920, during the Red Scare, when fear of Bolshevism and anarchism was rampant, a bomb outside the building killed thirty-three people, injured hundreds more, and pockmarked the J. P. Morgan headquarters across the street. The bombers were never identified.

The New York exchange, known as the "Big Board" and the world's largest stock exchange, merged in 2007 with Euronext, which traces its roots over four centuries to the exchange in Amsterdam, established by the Dutch East India Company seven years before Henry Hudson arrived in the New World.

SECTION OF THE WATER PIPE
WITH IRON WATER GATE
LAID BY
THE MANHATTAN COMPANY

·17·

Water Pipe

A Legacy of Liquidity

New York could survive—even thrive—without being the nation's capital; it couldn't become a burgeoning metropolis without drinking water. Manhattan was surrounded by rivers, but they were brackish estuaries. When yellow fever threatened, beer was safer to drink than water. Alexander Hamilton's nemesis, Aaron Burr, appeared to come to the parched city's rescue, though even then Albany operated in mysterious ways. Burr wangled a charter from the state legislature in 1799 to supply the city with water through the Manhattan Company.

But Burr was keener on other liquid assets. Invoking an overlooked clause in the company's charter—which allowed a surplus to be invested in any enterprise—he created the Bank of the Manhattan Company to break the monopoly of Hamilton's Bank of New York. Burr's company raised $2 million, only 5 percent of which was spent on improving the water supply.

The bank would thrive, but the company spent only sparingly on wooden water pipes hollowed from tree trunks, pumps from less than pristine wells in swarming neighborhoods and downtown holding tanks (the original octagonal design for one Manhattan Company reservoir near City Hall uncannily anticipates Chase's logo, although the graphic designers say that's merely coincidental). By the end of 1801, twenty miles of pipe served about fourteen hundred homes.

The company's abject failure to supply the city with sufficient potable water—and several cholera epidemics, followed by the Great Fire of 1837—led city officials to construct the innovative Croton Reservoir system, which drew from lakes, dams, and aqueducts in northern Westchester. The Old Croton Aqueduct, which took five years to build, delivered water to the city forty-one miles south by gravity (which is one reason so many nineteenth-century walk-up tenements were limited to about six stories—the maximum that the water could reach without additional pumps). On opening day in 1842, President John Tyler was on hand to witness a plume from the Croton-fed City Hall fountain surge fifty feet high. John B. Jervis was the visionary chief engineer who oversaw construction of the pipes, the tunnels, the receiving reservoir in Central Park, and the fortress-like distributing reservoir where the New York Public Library now stands on Fifth Avenue and Forty-Second Street.

Burr's Bank would evolve into Chase Manhattan (now JPMorgan Chase), which, fearful of jeopardizing its original charter, would regularly pump water from its downtown well near the Municipal Building until the 1920s.

·18·

Dueling Pistols

Climaxing Two Careers

As episodic rivals for financial influence and political power, Aaron Burr and Alexander Hamilton seemed fated for some fatal finale. Hamilton firmly believed in the right to bear arms, but as a check on the federal government's political and military muscle, not so people could go around shooting each other (though his own son was killed in a duel in 1801). Yet that is exactly what happened when Hamilton was challenged to a duel by Burr in the culmination of a long-standing feud between Hamilton's Federalists and Burr's Democratic-Republicans. The feud was stoked earlier in 1804, when Burr blamed Hamilton for his defeat in his campaign for governor of New York and focused on an unelaborated "despicable opinion" that Hamilton supposedly expressed. If Hamilton didn't deserve the blame, he would have welcomed it, having previously denounced Burr as, among other things, "a profligate, a voluptuary in the extreme."

Burr hoped a duel would revive his career. Hamilton was honor-bound to accept the challenge, which he did begrudgingly. To skirt New York's ban on dueling, on July 11, 1804, they rowed (in separate boats) to Weehawken (dueling was illegal in New Jersey as well but was prosecuted less aggressively).

Hamilton fired first, the historian Joseph J. Ellis concluded, "but he aimed to miss Burr, sending his ball into the tree above and behind Burr's location." Burr returned the fire and, intentionally or not, mortally wounded Hamilton. He was indicted for murder in both New York and New Jersey but never convicted.

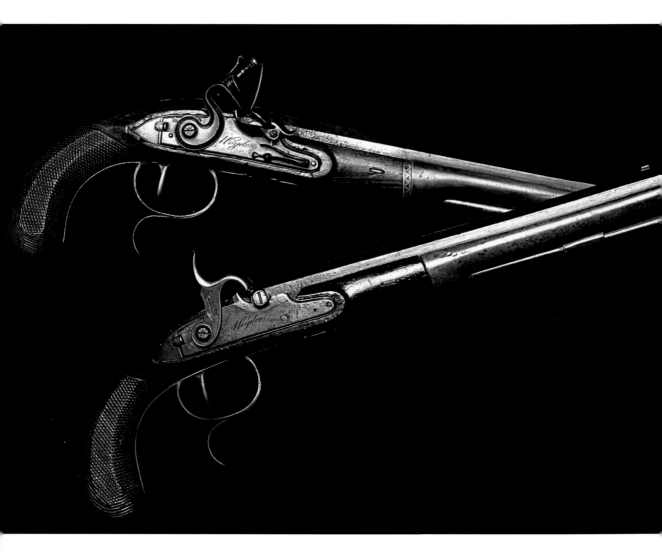

Hamilton died the next day in Manhattan. The duel also proved fatal to Burr's political career (although the .56-caliber pistols, which belonged to Hamilton's brother-in-law, wound up with the winner: They are displayed on the client dining floor at the Park Avenue headquarters of JPMorgan Chase).

Burr would never again hold elective office. He became a pariah who lived in relative obscurity. Pressed for cash in 1833, when he was seventy-seven, he married Eliza Jumel, a former prostitute whose Morris-Jumel Mansion in Washington Heights was where George Washington maintained his headquarters after fleeing the British downtown in the fall of 1776. The mansion is also Manhattan's oldest surviving house. Jumel's property would later be intersected by the Croton Aqueduct, built to convey the fresh water from Westchester that Burr's Manhattan Company was never able to supply sufficiently from its wells downtown.

·19·

Missing

The Birth of Literary Hype

The message at the bottom of the third column of the October 26, 1809, edition of the *New York Evening Post* ominously began with a single word: "Distressing." The following two paragraphs amounted to a missing persons notice, informing readers that a "small elderly gentleman, dressed in an old black coat and cocked hat," had left his lodgings some time ago and "has not since been heard of."

The advertisement cautioned that, "as there are some reasons for believing he is not entirely in his right mind and as great anxiety is entertained about him," any information about him would be appreciated at "the Columbian Hotel on Mulberry Street." The ad ended with a postscript: "Printers of Newspapers would be aiding the cause of humanity" by republishing the notice. Subsequent notices elaborated that the missing man, named Knickerbocker, had been spotted by passengers on the Albany stagecoach near Kings Bridge, holding "a small bundle tied in a red bandana," and that he had left in his lodgings "a very curious kind of a written book" that the hotel proprietor would have to sell to collect his back rent. True to his word, the proprietor published the book on December 6, 1809.

Humanity undoubtedly benefited from the discovery of Diedrich Knickerbocker's book, *History of New-York, from the Beginning of the World to the End of the Dutch Dynasty,* but the chief beneficiary was Washington Irving. Under the guise of his narrator, the fictional Knickerbocker, Irving not only fertilized New York's Dutch roots for a city struggling with its own identity; he also helped establish the city as a cultural mecca. At the same time, he perpetrated a fabulous literary hoax that became a paradigm for public relations in the publishing industry.

In 1809 New Yorkers were celebrating the bicentennial of Henry Hudson's voyage of discovery, but were still suffering an identity crisis after the Founding Fathers had transplanted the nation's capitol to the Potomac. Irving supplied that identity. As a cleverly satirical twenty-six-year-old, he supplanted the dominant Yankee hierarchy and created a brand that would be perpetuated over the course of two centuries in beers, hotels, baggy-kneed pants, and a heartbreaking basketball team.

DISTRESSING.

*** Left his lodgings some time since, and has not since been heard of, a small elderly gentleman, dressed in an old black coat and cocked hat, by the name of KNICKERBOCKER. As there are some reasons for believing he is not entirely in his right mind, and as great anxiety is entertained about him, any information concerning him left either at the Columbian Hotel, Mulberry-street, or at the Office of this paper will be thankfully received.

P. S. Printers of Newspapers would be aiding the cause of humanity, in giving an insertion to the above.

Oct. 26   3t

Irving's Knickerbocker, whose surname name was borrowed from an upstate family, provided the historical foundation, real or imagined, on which the New York mythos would thrive (Irving also popularized St. Nicholas, chimney and all). The "shabby and superior, iconic and intellectual, purveyor of 'fake history' nearly two centuries before Jon Stewart" was Irving's vehicle, wrote his biographer, Elizabeth A. Bradley. Irving, she added, was "not just the first writer to identify and exploit the market," but "his narrator became a market in and of itself." It was also Irving who in 1807 bestowed on New York the nickname "Gotham," after the fabled English village whose ingenious inhabitants behaved so bizarrely in the early twelfth century that, rather than expropriate the townspeople's property, King John and his tax collectors bypassed the place altogether. (No reflection on out-of-towners, but the town inspired this immortal truth: "More fools pass through Gotham than remain in it.")

"What constitutes a New Yorker?" a *New York Times* headline inquired in 1907, a century after Irving's history was published. The article was illustrated with an oversize portrait of Father Knickerbocker.

·20·

Surveyor's Bolt

How Gridlock Began

You're more likely to trip over it than to hail it as a historical artifact, but that four-inch-high bolt protruding from a striated boulder in Central Park holds the key to what Rem Koolhaas would call Manhattan's "three-dimensional anarchy." If the nation's second-largest metropolis is the City of Angels, New York is the City of Angles—a rigid, no-frills 90-degree street grid that avoided the narrow, crooked, Dutch-inspired downtown streets that fed conflagration and disease. Instead, the grid spurred unprecedented development and spawned defiant jaywalking, taxicab geometry, and vehicular gridlock (a term popularized during the 1980 transit strike by Sam Schwartz, who became the city Traffic Department's chief engineer).

Thank John Randel, Jr., the visionary city surveyor hired by street commissioners sanctioned by the state. In 1811, when New York City barely bulged above what became Houston Street (not for nothing was it called North Street then), Randel fancifully but meticulously mapped a two-thousand-block matrix on forests, farms, salt marshes, country estates, and common lands north for nearly eight miles to what would become West 155th Street. (In 1846, Randel would be among the first to propose an elevated railway over Broadway.)

Randel's inexorable northward march was greeted ambivalently. He was vilified by everyone from Clement Clark Moore—who, before making a fortune parceling out his Chelsea estate and staking claim to "A Visit from St. Nicholas," branded the street commissioners "men who would have cut down the seven hills of Rome"—to Henry James, who later condemned the grid as a "primal topographic curse."

"To some, it may be a matter of surprise that the whole island has not been laid out as a city," the commissioners wrote. "To others it may be a subject of merri-

ment that the commissioners have provided space for a greater population than is collected at any spot on this side of China." They forecast that the 1811 city of some 60,000 would mushroom to 400,000 in fifty years, but by 1860, New York was bursting with more than double that number.

Historians have called his nine-foot-long map "the single most important document in New York City's development." Its geometric embodiment of Cartesian coordinates created a high-stakes chessboard. It paved the way for rational development, driving streets through private property (of the nearly two thousand buildings north of Houston Street, over a third had to be razed or transplanted) and imposing flat equal lots as a great leveler. The grid would prove surprisingly resilient, eventually accommodating motor vehicles, sidewalks, stoops, two thousand additional acres of landfill, superblocks like Lincoln Center, Rockefeller Center, and the Hudson Yards, and the most striking example of urban ideality, Central Park.

Randel crafted his own tools, filled field books with hundreds of pages of detailed notes and sketches, and to mark the intersections he envisioned, installed 1,549 three-foot-high marble monuments and, where the ground was too rocky, 98 iron bolts secured by lead. Nowhere, wrote Edward K. Spann, an urban historian, "was the triumph of the grid as decisive as in America's greatest city." At least one of those bolts remains, peeking from a boulder in Central Park.

KEG
FROM WHICH GOVERNOR CLINTON
POURED THE WATER OF LAKE ERIE INTO THE ATLANTIC
— OCTOBER 26, 1825 —
ON THE COMPLETION OF THE ERIE CANAL

WATER

·21·

Water Keg

Lifting All Boats

For over 350 years, New York's commercial supremacy depended on its pre-eminence as a port. Three developments, all early in the nineteenth century, assured New York's maritime ascendancy.

The first, in 1807, was Robert Fulton's successful test of a steamboat. Steam power meant that sailings—across the ocean or from Manhattan to Brooklyn—were no longer at the mercy of the serendipitous winds.

Ten years later, the Black Ball Line announced that the first of its ships to adhere to a regular schedule would depart for Liverpool on January 5, 1818, no matter how much cargo or how many passengers were on board and no matter what the weather. The era of dependable transatlantic travel had begun.

On October 26, 1825, the canal boat *Seneca Chief* left Buffalo carrying a seemingly modest cargo: three green kegs specially adorned with painted eagles and containing only water from Lake Erie. The voyage had been envisioned in 1808, when the state legislature commissioned a survey of the water route west. Its most enduring champion was DeWitt Clinton, a clairvoyant New York City mayor who would be elected governor in 1817, the same year ground was finally broken for the Erie Canal.

The canal was an engineering marvel, 40 feet wide and 4 feet deep, its 83 locks lifting boats 568 feet from the Hudson River to Lake Erie. Engineers developed hydraulic cement that cured underwater and would be used extensively in building the Croton Aqueduct. A towpath along the bank allowed horses or mules to pull boats, which could haul thirty tons of cargo and reduce the trip to five reasonably pleasant days rather than as long as two weeks on a crowded, dusty stagecoach.

Eight days after the *Seneca Chief* left Buffalo in 1825, DeWitt Clinton—his vision originally denigrated as a "Big Ditch"—emptied the ceremonial kegs 360 miles east and south into the Atlantic Ocean in a majestic "marriage of the waters." Clinton confidently predicted to city officials that their exclusive connection between the Atlantic and the Great Lakes would mean "no limit to your lucrative extensions of trade and commerce."

But the canal was about more than commerce. It elevated New York into the nation's prime seaport and gateway to the nation's interior (eclipsing Baltimore, Boston, New Orleans, and Philadelphia). The Hudson became the river of empire, the canal its man-made thrust westward to deliver cargo and export the culture and politics of the nation's preeminent city. Today the Erie remains in service as the oldest continuously operating canal in the country.

·22·

Potato

The Harvest of Hunger

Just as New York changed the complexion and politics of the rest of the country, immigrants would change the face of New York.

That change had been occurring incrementally early in the nineteenth century, until whole fields of Irish Lumper potatoes began rotting, precipitating starvation, which was exacerbated by British feudal indifference or worse. By the time a prolonged famine ended about a decade later, an estimated million Irish men, women, and children had died from disease or hunger, while as many as another million emigrated to the United States. Three in four headed for New York. By 1850, more native-born Irish lived in New York than Dublin (New York is still home to more people of Irish ancestry than the Irish capital). They would comprise the first wave of poor immigrants to America who would alter the nation's economic, political, and cultural cast.

Young Irish men and women left Ireland in the late 1840s for other reasons, too, but the potato blight became the most pressing. As much as three fourths of the crop was infected, inflicting horrific hardship. By 1847, about 50,000 Irish had landed in New York (as had an equal number of German immigrants). But with about 375,000 residents then, or about three times the population of Boston, New

York was somewhat better able to absorb them. They were the vanguard of an immigrant influx that would increase the Irish share of the city's foreign-born population to nearly half. They are commemorated by the Irish Hunger Memorial in Battery Park City.

That Irish Catholics also transformed the city's religious demographic did not endear them to native-born Protestants. The Democratic organization came to see the wisdom of recruiting this vast influx of mostly illiterate foreigners into their political ranks, but the immigrants' most consistent champion was John J. Hughes, the Irish-born first archbishop of New York. He was known as "Dagger John," ostensibly because of the flourish of his signature (he drew a cross next to his name, which some regarded as a threatening dagger) but also because he would prove a dogged defender of his flock.

He founded what became Fordham University and the Catholic school system and laid the cornerstone for the majestic twin-spired St. Patrick's Cathedral on bucolic Fifth Avenue—a thumb in the eye of New York Protestants. He also bluntly expressed his eye-for-an-eye philosophy in a warning to the mayor during anti-Catholic rampages in other cities. Recalling the Russians' scorched-earth policy to thwart Napoleon, Hughes declared: "If a single Catholic Church were burned in New York, the city would become a second Moscow." Despite the growing political clout of immigrants, their children and grandchildren, the first Irish Catholic mayor—William R. Grace—would not be elected until 1880. Governor Alfred E. Smith, the grandson of Irish immigrants who settled on the Lower East Side, would be nominated for president in 1928 but would lose to Herbert Hoover after an anti-Catholic campaign.

The Irish Lumper potato, meanwhile, virtually vanished.

·23·

Sewing Machine

The Fabric Behind Manufacturing

Immigrants who built New York's roads, canals, and bridges also manned its factories, transforming the city into the nation's manufacturing capital in the nineteenth century. That distinction heavily influenced its initial predisposition against the Civil War, and then its robust economy, once war began.

Buoyed by Isaac M. Singer's marketing of the first commercially successful sewing machine in the 1850s and the shift in demand from tailor-made to ready-made clothing—first for slaves and then for Union soldiers—the garment industry boomed. In a marked metamorphosis, by the end of the war, more Americans were buying their clothing than making it themselves.

Making clothing was labor-intensive. It accounted for nearly one in three manufacturing jobs as early as 1860. The garment industry became the city's biggest employer, fueled by the influx of cheap Eastern European immigrant labor. By 1900, production by the second biggest industry, sugar refining, was valued at only one third that of the garment industry. A decade later, it was producing 40 percent of men's and 70 percent of women's clothing purchased across the country.

The garment industry also introduced women to the workplace and transformed Midtown West into the world's densest and most vibrant district for fashion design and manufacturing. Each block boasted its own specialty, from furriers to button-makers, trimmings, notions, and bridal gowns.

In recent decades, high Manhattan rents and cheaper nonunion labor in the South and in Asia have siphoned off most of the manufacturing. Many showrooms remain, and buyers still throng to Fashion Week in New York every February and September. But the Fashion Center Business Improvement District considered changing its name to reflect the growing diversity of tenants in the district bounded roughly by Thirty-Fourth to Forty-Second Streets and Fifth to Ninth Avenues.

Abraham Cahan, the socialist founder of the *Jewish Daily Forward*, wrote: "Foreigners ourselves, and mostly unable to speak English, we had Americanized the system of providing clothes for the American woman of moderate or humble means. The average American woman is the best-dressed woman in the world, and the Russian Jew has had a good deal to do with making her one."

Significantly, the clothing industry also emerged as an incubator for union organizers. The International Ladies' Garment Workers Union and the Amalgamated Clothing Workers were at the forefront of labor reforms, many of which were first adopted by New York early in the twentieth century and later became a template for New Deal labor and social welfare legislation nationally.

·24·

The Price of Admission

Riding into Destiny

Rosa Parks is hailed as "the first lady of civil rights" for triggering the Montgomery, Alabama, bus boycott. Elizabeth Jennings of New York, all but forgotten, beat her by over a century.

Jennings was the daughter of a freeborn black man and merchant tailor who lived on Church Street downtown. She taught full-time for $225 annually at the Board of Education's Colored School No. 5 on Thomas Street and volunteered Sundays as an organist at the First Colored American Congregational Church on Sixth Street.

On Sunday, July 16, 1854, late for church, she boarded a horse-drawn Third Avenue trolley car at Pearl and Chatham Streets, only to have the conductor order her off to await the next car (which, he explained, "had my people in it"). When she refused to disembark, he and the driver forcefully evicted her. "They then both seized hold of me by the arms and pulled and dragged me flat down on the bottom of the platform, so that my feet hung one way and my head the other, nearly on the ground," she recalled. "I screamed murder with all my voice." She also sued.

Blacks constituted about 14,000 of New York City's 515,000 residents then. Segregation was still very much the custom, and blacks were grappling with recent immigrants for the lowest rungs of the economic and social ladder. The trolley man was denounced by Jennings's supporters as a "ruffianly Irish driver," and the *Tri-*

bune questioned why respectable blacks should be "thrust from our public conveyances while German or Irish women, with a quarter of mutton or a load of codfish, can be admitted."

Civil rights advocates enlisted a twenty-four-year-old lawyer named Chester A. Arthur, who had written an anti-slavery treatise as a college student and would later become president of the United States. The case was tried on February 22, 1855, in Brooklyn, where the Third Avenue Railway Company had its headquarters. Arthur reminded the judge that a new state law made common carriers liable for their agents' acts, and the judge so instructed the jury, adding, according to one account, "that colored persons, if sober, well-behaved and free from disease, had the same rights as others." The jury agreed, awarding Jennings $225 (the judge added 10 percent, plus costs), which was about half of what she had sued for, but equal to her full year's salary. The ruling apparently set a precedent. Four years later, the Eighth Avenue Railroad Company settled with a black Sunday school superintendent who had been beaten and evicted from a trolley and agreed to integrate its cars.

In 1863, Jennings dodged the Draft Riots to bury her one-year-old son in Cypress Hills Cemetery in Brooklyn. She later opened the first kindergarten for black children in her home at 237 West Forty-First Street. Jennings would live to see a state civil rights act passed in 1873. Because of her courage, one historian later wrote, "the sounds of the river could not be stilled."

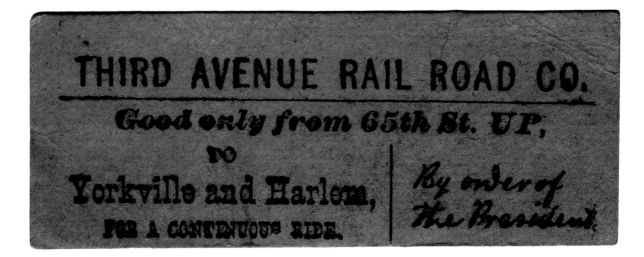

·25·

Republican Ticket

The Speech Heard 'Round the World

The six-foot-four midwesterner took the ferry from New Jersey and loped up Broadway to his lodgings at the Astor House across from City Hall. He was in town to deliver a speech, the venue for which had been shifted to Cooper Union from Plymouth Church in leafy Brooklyn Heights. He boarded another ferry for the obligatory visit to hear Henry Ward Beecher deliver his Sunday sermon there. He also dropped by City Hall, a den of Southern sympathy and pro-cotton lobbyists, anti-abolitionism, and talk of secession by the nation's largest city. On Monday, February 27, 1860, before delivering his first speech in the east—a speech that would transform him from a regional phenomenon into a national political figure—he bought a new top hat from Knox at Fulton Street and dropped by Mathew Brady's temporary studio at Bleecker Street to sit for (actually, he was photographed standing up, to reflect his full stature) a likeness that would introduce him to the nation in a first political portrait.

In the annals of American political oratory, few speeches rival Abraham Lincoln's presidential audition at Cooper Union that night in eloquence and impact. The hall sat eighteen hundred and was only three quarters filled, but the speech, in which the fifty-one-year-old Lincoln contrarily declared that "right makes might," would be reprinted and disseminated to every corner of the country. Lincoln's goal was twofold: to unequivocally denounce slavery and to improve his party's odds in the 1860 presidential campaign. He managed to win the plaudits of New York's Republican newspapers and outflank the state's favorite son, William H. Seward, for the nomination later that year (he also collected an impressive two-hundred-dollar fee). His performance would blunt expected Democratic margins in the city sufficiently to deliver New York State and its trove of electoral votes to Lincoln that November. (With typical understatement, he wrote his wife a few days after the speech that it "went off passably well.")

Organizers of the speech were competing with other offerings that night, including a performance by Jenny Lind, P. T. Barnum's "Swedish Nightingale," at the Winter Garden. The Cooper Union tickets were twenty-five cents, and apparently, only one survives. It was bought at auction in 2005 by Edward Gillette, a Kansas City, Kansas, criminal defense and personal injury lawyer whose great-great-grandfather served as a Union officer during the Civil War.

Cooper Union would figure twice more in Lincoln what-ifs. According to some uncorroborated accounts, the morning after his speech, Erastus Corning, a director of the New York Central, offered Lincoln an astounding ten thousand dollars a year to be the railroad's lawyer. "If Lincoln had accepted his offer," Edward Hun-

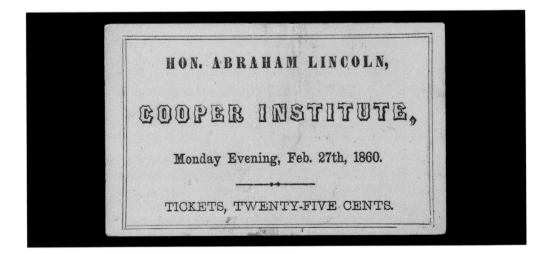

HON. ABRAHAM LINCOLN,

COOPER INSTITUTE,

Monday Evening, Feb. 27th, 1860.

TICKETS, TWENTY-FIVE CENTS.

gerford wrote in *Men and Iron,* "he unquestionably would have declined the presidency of the United States."

Twice more he was invited to speak at Cooper Union but declined. The last time was at an April 11, 1865, meeting to commemorate the attack on Fort Sumter. Had he attended, he probably would have been unable to return to Washington in time for the Good Friday performance at Ford's Theatre that ended his life.

"Cooper Union was not just a speech," Harold Holzer, a Lincoln scholar, wrote. "It was a conquest—a public relations triumph, a political coup d'état within the Republican party, and an image transfiguration abetted by the press and illustrated by the most felicitous photo opportunity in American history."

·26·

Otis Safety Brake

New York Rising

In one form or another, elevators date to the third century B.C., although the most famous may have been one installed at Versailles in 1743 so King Louis XV of France could consort more easily with his mistress who lived one flight up.

More often than not, they were originally built for freight, lifted by animals and humans (an easier task when counterweights were included) and later by steam, by hydraulic power pushing a piston, and by electricity. Elisha Otis didn't invent the elevator, but he made it safe enough for everyday use. Without his safety brake, skyscrapers never would have been practical.

The Vermont-born inventor was working as a mechanic for Josiah Maize's bedstead company in nearby Yonkers when he began tinkering with a hoisting device that could lift heavy machinery to the upper floor of Maize & Burns's factory. He devised an "improvement in hoisting apparatus elevator brake," not the most flashy-sounding invention, but one that revolutionized urban development.

Among those who realized its potential was P. T. Barnum, the museum, circus, and theatrical impresario, who was president of the Crystal Palace in what is now Bryant Park. In 1854, during the Exposition of the Industry of All Nations, he introduced "the first elevator wherein provision was made for stopping the fall of the car in the contingency of the breaking of the hoisting cables." In a death-defying demonstration of vertical engineering beneath the Crystal Palace's hundred-foot diameter dome, Otis had himself hoisted to the top of the building, where he dramatically ordered an assistant to sever the elevator cables with a saber. Crowds screamed as the car dropped for a few seconds. But instead of plummeting to the floor, the cab was safely stopped by a spring-loaded mechanism that meshed with the sawtoothed guide rails flanking the shaft. "All safe, ladies and gentlemen," he reassured the crowd. "All safe."

In 1857 Elisha Otis and the Otis Elevator Company began manufacturing passenger elevators. The first public elevator, a steam-powered hydraulic passenger model, was installed on March 23, 1857, by Otis in the five-story cast-iron E. V.

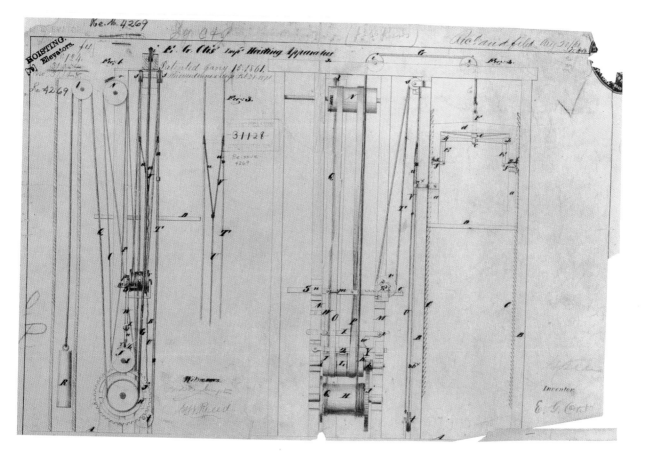

Haughwout & Co. department store at Broome Street and Broadway in what is now SoHo. While the building was under eighty feet tall, Eder V. Haughwout figured, correctly, that an innovative elevator would attract curious customers. United States Patent No. 31,128 was issued less than three months before Otis died in 1861.

In 1870 the 130-foot-high steel-framed and elevator-equipped Equitable Building, at 120 Broadway, ushered in the skyscraper era and the vertical city. Otis became a brand name, and the company's elevators were installed in landmarks that included the Eiffel Tower, the Chrysler Building, and the Empire State Building. In 1899 the company introduced the moving stairs, known as the escalator, drawing on the work of several inventors, including Jesse W. Reno, whose "endless conveyor" or "inclined elevator" was installed at the Old Iron Pier at Coney Island in 1896 and later that year on the Manhattan side of the Brooklyn Bridge.

·27·

Draft Wheel

The Civil War at Home

Congress passed the first federal conscription act in 1863, applying to men between twenty-five and forty-five. Exempted were draftees who could provide a substitute or pay a bounty of three hundred dollars. The first draft lottery was scheduled for July 11, a Saturday. By the following Monday, a mob of protesters had rampaged through the provost marshal's uptown headquarters at Third Avenue and Forty-Sixth Street in the prelude to the nation's bloodiest domestic uprising, except for the Civil War itself. At least 105 people died, with hundreds more soldiers, police officers, and civilians wounded. Order was restored four days later, after five Union regiments were summoned from Gettysburg and the Common Council, urged on by Boss Tweed, the Democratic ward-heeler, appropriated $2 million for poor draftees who could not afford to pay the $300 exemption fee.

The instrument that triggered the Draft Riots was innocuous enough. It was a small wooden barrel rotated with a crank and mounted on a bracket. The draft wheel (one for the Seventh Congressional District on the Lower East Side is in the collection of the New-York Historical Society) contained the names, addresses, and occupations of potential draftees.

Southern cotton was king in New York, as a commodity to be traded and shipped overseas and to be manufactured into finished clothing, towels, and other accessories. Under Mayor Fernando Wood, New York had even considered seceding in solidarity with the Confederacy and forming a sovereign Tri-Insula composed of Manhattan, Long Island, and Staten Island. The city was flush with import tariffs being diverted to Washington by the federal government. No surprise that Abe Lincoln lost New York City in 1860, although he carried New York State. Once war was declared, though, New York would furnish more draftees and volunteers than any other state.

·28·

City College Birthday

A Terrible Thing to Waste

It wasn't really a funeral, although the students billed it as one. It was more like a rebirth the day the Free Academy, founded in 1847, was rechristened in 1866 as the College of the City of New York.

The academy had been founded by Townsend Harris, a wealthy merchant and president of the board of education who recruited Horace Webster, a West Point graduate, to conduct an experiment in higher education. "The experiment is to be tried," Webster said, "whether the children of the people, the children of the whole people, can be educated; and whether an institution of the highest grade can be successfully controlled by the popular will, not by the privileged few." Webster stayed on to become the first president of City College.

It began as an all-male institution but was progressive in other ways, forming an academic senate in 1867 (billed as the first student government in the nation) and abolishing chapel attendance early in the twentieth century to make it more welcoming to non-Christian students. In 1907, after enrollment topped thirty-two thousand, the college moved to what would become a thirty-six-acre verdant neo-Gothic campus designed by George Browne Post. (Satel-

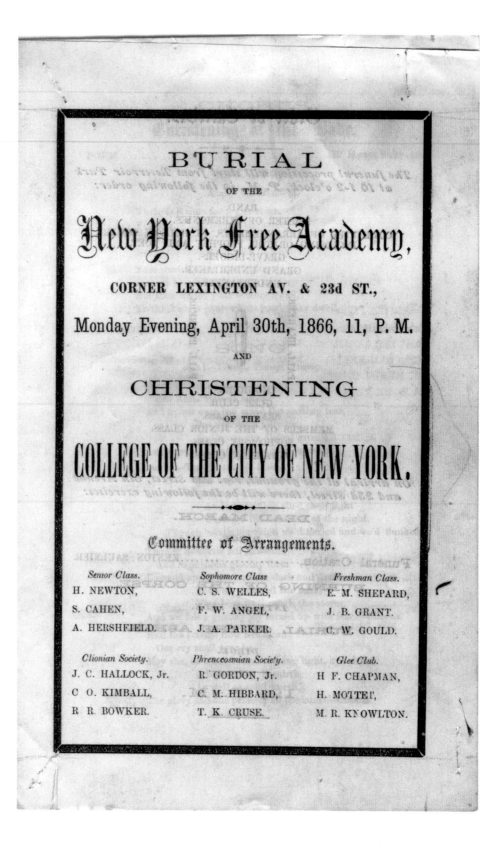

BURIAL

OF THE

𝔑𝔢𝔴 𝔜𝔬𝔯𝔨 𝔉𝔯𝔢𝔢 𝔄𝔠𝔞𝔡𝔢𝔪𝔶,

CORNER LEXINGTON AV. & 23d ST.,

Monday Evening, April 30th, 1866, 11, P. M.

AND

CHRISTENING

OF THE

COLLEGE OF THE CITY OF NEW YORK.

Committee of Arrangements.

Senior Class.	*Sophomore Class.*	*Freshman Class.*
H. NEWTON,	C. S. WELLES,	E. M. SHEPARD,
S. CAHEN,	F. W. ANGEL,	J. B. GRANT.
A. HERSHFIELD.	J. A. PARKER.	C. W. GOULD.

Clionian Society.	*Phrenocosmian Society.*	*Glee Club.*
J. C. HALLOCK, Jr.	R. GORDON, Jr.	H. F. CHAPMAN,
C. O. KIMBALL,	C. M. HIBBARD,	H. MOTTET,
R. R. BOWKER.	T. K. CRUSE.	M. R. KNOWLTON.

lite campuses would later become Brooklyn and Queens Colleges.) Women were admitted to graduate programs in 1930 and, finally, to the college in 1951.

City became known during the 1920s and '30s as "the poor man's Harvard" because, as the college's official history recalls, "in the years when top-flight private schools were restricted to the children of the Protestant establishment, thousands of brilliant individuals (including Jewish students) attended City College because they had no other option. . . . Even today, no other public college has produced as many graduates who went on to win Nobel Prizes; like City students today, they were the children of immigrants and the working class, and often the first of their families to go to college."

In the 1930s the college was a political cauldron dominated by Communists, socialists, Trotskyites, Stalinists, other radicals, and tamer progressives, some of whom would emerge decades later as the lapsed liberals who formed the core of neoconservatism. "The memory of poverty and those tedious subway rides has faded with time, whereas what I now recollect most vividly is the incredible vivacity with which we all confronted the dismal 1930s," wrote one of those old liberals, Irving Kristol, without regrets. "If I left City College with a better education than did many students at other and supposedly better colleges, it was because my involvement in radical politics put me in touch with people and ideas that prompted me to read and think and argue with a furious energy."

The twenty-four institutions of higher learning of the City University of New York constitute the largest public urban university system in the country. City, the founding institution, has been joined by ten senior colleges, seven community colleges, an honors college, and five graduate and professional schools, with a full-time enrollment of more than 160,000.

·29·

How the Library Began

Remember the Mane

In the 1930s, Mayor Fiorello H. La Guardia dubbed the twin marble lions guarding the New York Public Library on Fifth Avenue Patience and Fortitude. By any standard they would qualify as emblematic of a great cultural resource. But Michael Miscione, the Manhattan borough historian, has suggested something less photogenic but more transformative: Samuel J. Tilden's will. His bequest to establish and maintain a free public library in the city served, Miscione says, "to solidify the city's commitment to literacy, culture and a public-private partnership that enabled New York City to create so many world-class cultural institutions."

Tilden, the son of a patent medicine manufacturer, was a successful corporate lawyer, shrewd investor, political reformer, and anti-slavery Free Soil Democrat who would battle the abuses of Tammany Hall. He was elected governor of New York and in the disputed 1876 presidential campaign against Rutherford B. Hayes won a majority of the popular vote but lost the Electoral College (by one vote). "I can retire to public life," Tilden said, "with the consciousness that I shall receive from posterity the credit of having been elected to the highest position in the gift of the people, without any of the cares and responsibilities of the office."

New York had lots of libraries at the end of the nineteenth century, but most charged admission and were privately funded. Tilden left about $2.4 million (almost $100 million in today's dollars), the bulk of his fortune, to "establish and maintain a free library and reading room in the city of New York." The Tilden Trust was merged with the Astor (founded by John Jacob Astor, from his fur-trading fortune and presided over by Washington Irving) and Lenox (founded by the bibliophile James Lenox) libraries in 1895 to form the New York Public Library. The consolidation—orchestrated by John Bigelow, a lawyer for the Tilden Trust—was hailed, according to the library's official history, as "an unprecedented example of private philanthropy for the public good." Six years later, Andrew Carnegie agreed to donate more than $5 million to establish sixty-five branch libraries under the proviso that they be maintained by the city government. (Brooklyn and Queens are served by separate library systems.)

The New York Public Library's $9 million central research library, designed by Carrère and Hastings, opened in 1911 at Fifth Avenue and West Forty-Second Street on the site of the old Croton Distributing Reservoir. At the time, the beaux arts building was the largest marble structure in the United States. The original collection contained more than a million volumes; today it includes more than fifty million books and other items stored on-site, in stacks under Bryant Park and in a warehouse in Princeton, New Jersey. The New York Public is the second-largest public library in the United States (after the Library of Congress) and the world's third-largest. The central research branch has been featured in numerous films, notably *Breakfast at Tiffany's, You're a Big Boy Now,* and *Ghostbusters,* and in books, including *The Rise of David Levinsky.*

Tilden never lost faith. Referring to his 1876 defeat, his epitaph reads: "I Still Trust in The People."

·30·

Linotype

The Words of the Profits

What Johann Gutenberg did for literacy in Europe in the Middle Ages by inventing movable type, the Linotype machine accomplished four hundred years later for European immigrants in America. The Linotype was manufactured in Brooklyn, where its introduction had profound consequences not only for journalism but also for organized labor. Thomas Edison called the machine the Eighth Wonder of the World, and an 1889 edition of *The Manufacturer and Builder* described it as "a remarkable triumph of inventive ingenuity."

Previously, type was set by hand, one character at a time, a process that was both slow and highly labor-intensive for an army of compositors. It meant daily newspapers were generally limited to eight pages. The Linotype—short for a line of type—was a 250-cubic-foot Rube Goldberg–looking contraption invented and perfected by Ottmar Mergenthaler, a German immigrant watchmaker and machine shop operator who introduced it in 1884 after being inspired by a note-taking system that a stenographer for Lincoln's presidential cabinet was trying to perfect.

Using brass matrices for each character—much like the Springerle Christmas cookie mold Mergenthaler once made for his mother—the machine converted molten lead into complete lines of type, justified for a specified column width and set by an operator at a 90-character (originally 107) keyboard. The type was fitted into a mold the size of the newspaper page and was then used to form the metal plates from which papers were printed.

The Linotype allowed for more pages, quicker delivery of news, and dissemination of information to more and more readers. No city was a bigger newspaper town than New York. By 1865, one in eight editions of newspapers in the United States were being published there, and five years later, after ground wood pulp, or "brittle paper," was introduced, ninety newspapers were being published in the city alone. (The first regular comic was Richard Felton Outcalt's *Yellow Kid,* which

appeared in the *Sunday World* in 1895, and the most famous editorial appeared two years later in *The Sun,* "Is There a Santa Claus?," in response to a letter from young Virginia O'Hanlon of 115 West Ninety-Fifth Street.)

Linotypes, manufactured on Ryerson Street in Fort Greene, Brooklyn, were in regular use for nearly a century and profoundly influenced the labor movement—first when they were introduced (one operator could do the work of three to six compositors) and later, when they became obsolete (the shift to "cold type," in effect set digitally by the reporter or editor using a keyboard and a computer screen).

·31·

Water Tanks

Gravity Goes Only So Far

New York's gravity-fed water supply system from reservoirs up to 125 miles upstate generally flows roughly six stories high once it reaches the city. In taller buildings, to maintain constant pressure, water has to be pumped to rooftop tanks to supply tenants and to assist firefighters.

As many as fifteen thousand wooden tanks punctuate the skyline, built largely by two family-owned companies, Rosenwach Group and Isseks Brothers, both of which have been in business since the late nineteenth century (a third company, American Pipe and Tank Lining, has maintained tanks for three generations).

The cylindrical tanks, which typically measure about twelve feet high and twelve feet across and are topped by a conical enclosure, hold ten thousand gallons on average and cost about thirty thousand dollars. Tap water is siphoned off the top, while murkier bottom water, mixed with sediment, is reserved for firefighting. As in a toilet tank, a ballcock regulates the level. The tanks can be dismantled and replaced in as little as twenty-four hours and take about three hours to fill.

They are usually made of wood because it is less susceptible to changes in temperature, cheaper, and, with proper maintenance, should last around three decades. No paint or adhesive is used; the wood expands when moistened and seals itself. The individual cedar or California redwood staves (easy to transport to the roof in a freight elevator) are encircled by galvanized steel hoops to keep them from bursting.

The tanks are not unique to New York, but nowhere else have they become such natural features of the cityscape, like outdoor furniture on a suburban patio. No wonder they appear in Edward Hopper's soulful paintings and Saul Steinberg's iconic New Yorker's myopic worldview. They have been sanctioned by city planners as an architectural rooftop amenity—operative or not—in Manhattan's Tribeca neighborhood ("naked power," the architect Robert A. M. Stern characterized those tanks, as opposed to rooftop reservoirs that are camouflaged or enclosed) and elevated into folk art (a hollow plastic version was even installed on the roof of the Museum of Modern Art).

How long the tanks will remain a fixture of the skyscraper will depend on how fast developers switch to steel tanks, which are more expensive and potentially impart a metallic taste to the water, or high-pressure pumps, which obviate the need for tanks altogether.

Meanwhile, the family-owned firms that build and service the tanks are thriving. "It's kind of in our blood," said Henry Rosenwach, who joined the firm at a propitious moment after graduating from Vanderbilt University. "I think," he recalled, "it was at the point when it was time for me to get a job."

·32·

Tweed's Secret Accounts

The Reformation

Willliam Magear Tweed had a ring to his name. Once he relinquished his honorary role as a volunteer fireman (he was presented with a trumpet, which heralded his even more visible role), the corpulent caricature of a party boss became a congressman, then wielded enormous political power as the grand sachem of Tammany Hall. The corrupt machine controlled mid-nineteenth-century New York by reliably delivering the votes of Irish and other immigrants to deserving Democratic candidates and, in return, doling out patronage (in the form of government jobs, protection from an aggressive police force, and Christmas turkeys).

For helping Jay Gould and James Fisk, Jr., retain control of the Erie Railroad, Tweed was named a director of the line and further enriched himself by following their advice on investments. But once complacent city fathers concluded that Tweed's financial machinations threatened New York's creditworthiness, he was arrested for corruption and political misconduct. The degree of his graft was exposed by *The New York Times,* which rejected a $5 million bribe (about $100 million in today's dollars) to bury its findings. "I don't think," responded George Jones, the editor, "the devil will ever make a higher bid for me than that."

Instead, beginning July 22, 1871, the *Times* published "The Secret Accounts" on its front pages, an item-by-item litany of overpriced purchases and kickbacks for the lavish new courthouse that Tweed and his cronies built just behind City Hall. (The courthouse was so massive that during New York's fiscal crisis in the mid-1970s, the city couldn't even afford to raze the derelict building.)

"The following accounts, copied with scrupulous fidelity" from the comptroller's books, filled half the front page, a ledger of 136 items specified to the penny ($2,870,464.06, or $53 million in today's dollars, for repairs by a contractor whom the *Times* dubbed "The Prince of Plasterers"). They spelled Tweed's demise. The *Times* demonstrated that although the invoices supposedly were submitted by a dozen companies, all the money was funneled to Ingersoll & Co., a business belonging to a Tweed family friend. Tweed cronies supplied $565,000 worth of carpets—enough to carpet City Hall Park three times over. *Times* editorials not

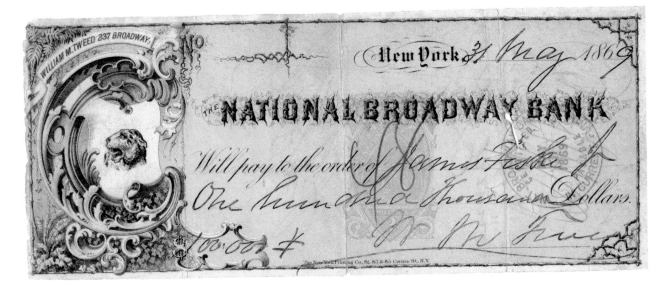

only accused the ring of corruption but indicted the city fathers who—like the bankers and credit-rating agencies a century later—had complicitly given the city's suspect finances their blessing and looked the other way as long as their own interests were protected.

The *Times* also coupled verbatim evidence with editorials and published pamphlets detailing the frauds and an entire edition in German to reach the city's largest non-English-speaking immigrant group. Tweed was also "doomed by cartoon." The *Times*'s exposé was coupled with devastating caricatures by Thomas Nast in *Harper's Weekly*.

Tweed was imprisoned, and escaped after a year but was rearrested. He died in 1878 in the Ludlow Street Jail on the Lower East Side. The jail is now the site of the Seward Park campus, which houses five city high schools run by the Department of Education, whose headquarters is in the old Tweed Courthouse on Chambers Street.

·33·

Atlantic Cable

A Digital Revolution

Captain Nemo witnessed it from the *Nautilus*. It snaked beneath the Atlantic to wreak havoc among Hans Christian Andersen's nautical creatures in "The Great Sea-Serpent." Henry James invoked it in *The American* when an American businessman announced his marriage.

The serpentine transatlantic cable was inaugurated on August 16, 1858. Four years earlier, Cyrus Field, a former dry goods clerk at the A. T. Stewart department store, teamed up with other New York investors and inventors, including Peter Cooper (who had built the first steam locomotive, founded Cooper Union for the Advancement of Science, and run for president); Abram Hewitt (Cooper's son-in-law, who would become mayor of New York); Samuel F. B. Morse (who perfected the telegraph), and Moses Taylor (who controlled what became Citibank), to connect telegraph lines in the first leg of their transatlantic venture, which would link Trinity Bay, Newfoundland, with Valencia, Ireland. The first message didn't arrive at supersonic speed, but it opened the door to instant communication between Europe and North America, which would cement New York's role as the nation's communications capital.

Queen Victoria sent the first telegram, hailing the cable as "an additional link between the nations whose friendship is founded on their common interest and reciprocal esteem." Her eighty-eight-word message took seventeen hours to transmit, or about one word every ten minutes. (President James Buchanan responded by proclaiming the telegraph cable "an instrument destined by Divine Providence to diffuse religion, civilization, liberty and law throughout the world.")

The cable failed within a month, but Field succeeded eight years later, immediately after the Civil War, with a circuit that could transmit at a breakneck speed of eight words a minute. The 1868 exchange of messages included the obligatory congratulations but added a tantalizing hint of the cable's potential influence on politics and financial markets: "Treaty of peace signed between Prussia and Austria."

The impact on journalism was powerful, on stock trading even more so. Suddenly, Wall Street and European exchanges could engage in what passed for instantaneous communication compared to the pokey ten days that news would have taken to travel by ship. Field's achievement would be followed ninety years later by the first telephone cable and, fifty years after that, by a fiber-optic link that accelerated communication by a competitive six milliseconds.

·34·

Dynamo

The Light at First Dawn

America's electric age was born at 257 Pearl Street in Lower Manhattan when Thomas Edison began operating the city's first central power station. His first dynamo, or generator, was built for the Paris Electrical Exposition of 1881 and began commercial operation at the Pearl Street plant on September 4, 1882.

Competitors had already installed harsh electric arc lights on Broadway from Fourteenth Street to Thirty-Fourth Street and on the Brooklyn Bridge, which opened in 1883. By 1890, more than thirty companies were generating or distributing electricity in New York City and Westchester, the territory that would be served by the Consolidated Edison Co.

Financed by J. P. Morgan and the Vanderbilts, Edison perfected a carbon filament that would burn in a glass bulb for as long as forty hours. He incorporated the Edison Electric Illuminating Company of New York to transform the novelty— a few private residences, like Morgan's, had self-contained power plants—into a commercially viable enterprise dependent on dynamos, voltage regulators, fuses, sockets, meters, switches, and miles of copper wire.

At 3:00 P.M. that September 4, Edison and his board of directors traveled about a half mile to Morgan's Wall Street office. With their watches synchronized, an engineer closed the circuit breaker at the plant; Edison flipped a switch; and the office was bathed in electric light. Under a month later, Edison had fifty-nine customers.

Each of the six dynamos weighed 27 tons—the largest ever built at the time— and produced enough direct current (100 kilowatts) to power 1,100 lightbulbs. The six giant dynamos (nicknamed Jumbo, after Barnum's elephant) were connected directly to a steam engine and became the prototype for generating power from a central station to distribute electricity to homes, a goal Edison had harbored for four years (blame Edison, too, for the first electric bill, based on his electrolytic meter).

Within a year or two, Edison's company was supplying more than five hundred customers. A fire destroyed the plant in 1890, but Dynamo No. 9 survived and continued operating until 1893. Today it is on exhibition at the Henry Ford historical attraction at Greenfield Village in Dearborn, Michigan.

The Institute for Electrical and Electronics Engineers describes the Pearl Street plant as the first "complete system of commercial electric lighting and power." The success of Edison's incandescent bulb created a demand for reliable power sources. "It was this demand," the institute concluded, "that led to the construction of the Pearl Street station and launched the modern electric utility industry" by generating reliable power and distributing it efficiently "at a price that competed with gas lighting."

·35·

Toll Ticket

Crossing Brooklyn Bridge

And if you believe that, I have a bridge to sell you." The expression evokes only one bridge, the Brooklyn. Probably no other bridge has been sold so many times to unsuspecting tourists, proving W. C. Fields's enduring adage that "you can't cheat an honest man." (Early in the twentieth century, at least two con men, William McCloundy and George Parker, were sentenced to Sing Sing for selling the bridge, an even more potentially profitable purchase before tolls were abolished in 1911.)

Whatever designs confidence men had on the bridge and its neo-Gothic granite towers, it had been envisioned by urban planners and civic leaders for decades. The culmination of political and mechanical engineering feats, when it finally opened on May 24, 1883, it linked two separate cities—New York and Brooklyn (then the fourth largest behind New York, Chicago, and Philadelphia)—and would speed the consolidation of Greater New York into a single city fifteen years later. Each city's ambivalence about the link was reflected in the original evenhanded names: the New York and Brooklyn Bridge and the East River Bridge. But city officials formally named it for Brooklyn in 1915, two years after the adjacent Manhattan Bridge was completed.

The bridge was designed by John Roebling, but his fatal injuries left construction in the hands of his son, Washington, and Washington's wife, Emily. Construction took fourteen years, involved six hundred workers daily, and cost $15 million (over $360 million in today's dollars). Its main span stretching 1,595.5 feet, it was the longest suspension bridge in the world, until it was overtaken by the Williamsburg Bridge in 1903. A few days after it opened, a stampede precipitated by a panic that it might collapse led to the death of at least twelve people. A year later, P. T. Barnum scotched doubts about the bridge's durability by leading Jumbo and twenty other elephants across the span.

Originally, a central elevated walkway for pedestrians was flanked by roadways for horse-drawn traffic, streetcars, and elevated trains between Sands Street in Brooklyn and Park Row in Manhattan. Just ten days before the formal opening, bridge trustees imposed fares of one cent for people on foot, five cents for railway passengers, and rates that ranged from two cents for a sheep to ten cents for a horse and wagon. Tolls were abolished in 1911 by Mayor William J. Gaynor, who declared, "I see no more reason for toll gates on the bridges than for toll gates on Fifth Avenue or Broadway."

On an average weekday, the bridge now carries about 120,000 vehicles and thousands more pedestrians. "When the Brooklyn Bridge was opened," Mayor George B. McClellan, Jr., declared two decades later, "Greater New York was born."

Sonnets.

I.

The New Colossus.

Not like the brazen Giant of Greek
With conquering limbs astride from
Here at our sea-washed sunset gates
A mighty woman with a torch, to
Is the imprisoned lightning, and her
Mother of Exiles. From her beacon-
Glows world-wide welcome; her mild
The air-bridged harbor that twin

·36·

New Colossus

A Rhyme Gives a Reason

America begins in New York," Kenneth T. Jackson, the Columbia University historian, likes to say. New York's tolerance for or, at least, indifference to diversity spread west to the rest of the country. Embodied by the Statue of Liberty, that philosophy defined America to the rest of the world through accounts that immigrants sent home.

In 1830, fewer than one in ten New Yorkers were foreign-born. Within two decades, nearly half were. Yet when the statue was dedicated in 1886 (six years before Ellis Island opened), the only immigrants mentioned were the "illustrious descendants of the French nobility" who had fought on behalf of the United States against Britain during the American Revolution.

Her official name was *Liberty Enlightening the World,* and her donor's agenda was to burnish France's republican roots after the oppressive reign of Napoléon III and to foster stronger bonds with America. But it was the words of a fourth-generation American whose father was a wealthy sugar refiner and whose great-great-uncle welcomed George Washington to Newport, Rhode Island, that almost single-handedly—if belatedly—transformed the monumental statue in New York Harbor into a "Mother of Exiles" who beckoned generations of immigrants.

Emma Lazarus's "New Colossus," with its memorable appeal to "give me your tired, your poor," was commissioned for a fund-raising campaign to pay for the statue's pedestal. Lazarus accepted the commission begrudgingly—few poets relish the idea of writing on deadline. But she was stirred by a wave of pogroms against Jews in Russia and by her regular visits to poor immigrants housed in temporary shelters on Wards Island. Lazarus wrote the sonnet in 1883, having seen only the torch when it was on display in Madison Square Park.

"It was a moment of moral and spiritual recovery, after her attempts to raise money to benefit the Russian-Jewish refugees of 1881–82 had largely fallen on deaf ears," said Esther Schor, her biographer and an English professor at Princeton University.

The sonnet would survive periodic efforts to excise Lazarus's reference to "wretched refuse" and would become enshrined in the political lexicon in the 1930s as an anthem for Americans who, with war again threatening in Europe, lobbied to reverse immigration quotas imposed a decade earlier.

Finally, in 1903, after relentless lobbying by Georgina Schuyler, a friend of Lazarus who was descended from Alexander Hamilton (himself an immigrant), it was affixed on a bronze tablet just inside the entrance to the pedestal. "An ex post facto inscription," as the art historian Marvin Trachtenberg wrote, that would elevate the values of immigration.

·37·

School Doorknob

Opening Young Minds

How best to symbolize New York City's commitment to free public education? What better entry-level totem than the brass knobs on classroom doors in elementary and secondary schools that date from the nineteenth to mid-twentieth centuries? They can still be found in some older schools and are available on eBay and in architectural salvage shops. (They were rendered anachronistic by the Americans with Disabilities Act, which required more accessible levers.) As one *New York Times* reader from California remembered, "They were heavy and ornate and functioned as billboards for the Board of Education." The knobs opened heavy oak doors that have beckoned generations of students since the movement for public funding to educate poor children was inaugurated in New York by the Free School Society (presided over by the ubiquitous DeWitt Clinton) in 1805 and a Board of Education was established in 1842 to provide nonsectarian public schooling (its Protestant bent prompted creation of a parallel Catholic system by Archbishop Hughes).

"Everywhere, at the beginning, the first schools were closely allied to the churches," former Mayor Seth Low wrote in his introduction to A. Emerson Palmer's history of the public system in 1904. In fact, Low wrote, the school established

for black children by the Manumission Society in 1787 "marked the first faint impulse towards free public education" (as well as the beginning of racial segregation, which would endure officially until 1900). That impulse evolved from an ideal of a free school for the poor to a public school for all.

Even in the early twentieth century, the system was not exactly universal. The schools superintendent promised that all students older than six would be enrolled, which would mean "it will be the first time in the modern history of New York's schools that there will have been no 'waiting list.'" (In a precursor to today's debate over pre-kindergarten classes, the *Times* carped, "A considerable number of mothers declared unhesitatingly that children not a day over four years old were more than six. Many mothers of foreign birth and with little realization of the purpose of public schools attempt every year to compel the schools to act as a sort of day nursery for them.")

Today, about 1.1 million students are enrolled in the city's public school system. With about four in ten living in households where a language other than English is spoken, the Department of Education translates report cards and other documents into Spanish, French, German, Chinese, Japanese, Urdu, Persian, Hindi, Russian, Bengali, Haitian Creole, Korean, and Arabic (but not, in a sign of changing demographics and social conventions, Italian, Yiddish, or Gaelic).

·38·

Ellis Island Manifest

Annie, We Hardly Knew Ye

Her two younger brothers elbowed her ahead of a burly German. A longshoreman shouted, "Ladies first." As a result, Annie Moore was presented with a ten-dollar gold coin and immortalized as the first immigrant to set foot on Ellis Island, on her fifteenth birthday, January 1, 1892.

The arrival was accurately reported, as was her gracious response to the gold piece presented by the nation's superintendent of immigration as the federal government assumed responsibility for supervising the influx of foreigners (before then, it was left largely to the states; New York welcomed them, more or less, at Castle Garden, in what is now Battery Park).

The true story of Annie Moore was discovered by genealogist Megan Smolenyak. Smolenyak (a genealogist's dream, she married a previously unrelated Smolenyak) teamed up with Brian G. Andersson, the New York City commissioner of records, to discover the iconic Moore in 2006.

Disembarking from steerage after twelve days on the steamship *Nevada* from Cobh, Ireland, Annie joined her parents, who had arrived several years earlier, in a five-story brick tenement at 32 Monroe Street in Manhattan. She later moved to a nearby apartment on the Bowery. Annie's father was a longshoreman. She married a bakery clerk. They had at least eleven children. Five survived to adulthood, and three had children of their own. She died of heart failure in 1924 at forty-seven. Her brother Anthony, who arrived with Annie, died in his twenties in the Bronx and was temporarily buried in a potter's field.

Annie lived and died within a few square blocks on the Lower East Side, where some of her descendants resided until recently. She is buried alongside the famous and forgotten in a Queens cemetery. Though she lived a poor immigrant's life, many of her descendants, who include an investment counselor and a PhD, prospered. "She sacrificed herself for future generations," Smolenyak said, describing Moore's descendants as "poster children" for immigrant America, with Irish, Jewish, Italian, and Scandinavian surnames. "It's an all-American family," she said. "Annie would have been proud."

As one guidebook says: "Annie Moore came to America bearing little more than her dreams; she stayed to help build a country enriched by diversity."

·39·

The Other Grand Central Clock

Making the Trains Run On Time

Say "Meet me at the clock," and everyone will find you at the famous four-faced opalescent glass timepiece atop the information booth in Grand Central Terminal. It's more famous than its sister clock in an archway in the Graybar Passage heading toward the Main Concourse, but the three words painted beneath make this otherwise undistinguished clock even more historic: "Eastern Standard Time." That the words are wrong almost eight months a year, during Daylight Saving Time, is irrelevant. They celebrate a phenomenon that began at Grand Central on a Sunday morning in 1883 and spread to every corner of the country—a uniformity imposed not by government but by frustrated timekeepers for most of the railroads that controlled nearly a hundred thousand miles of track across the continent.

Before Standard Time, noon was whenever—and wherever—the sun was farthest from the horizon, which meant when it was 12:12 in New York, it was 12:24

EASTERN STANDARD TIME

ENT

MAIN CONCOURSE

MTA Metro-North Railroad

JUST ARRIVED!
More New Ticket Vending Machines

TRACK 18

19 TRACKS

Train
Game

Metro-North Service
to Football Games at
the Meadowlands

in Boston, 12:07 in Philadelphia, and 11:17 in Chicago. The conflicts were intolerable, especially the crashes and missed connections blamed on unsynchronized minute hands. Solutions had been proposed for decades. The railroads finally embraced four time zones 15 degrees wide (the sun moves longitudinally 15 degrees an hour), as advocated by the Reverend Charles F. Dowd, co-principal of the ladies' seminary in Saratoga Springs that would become Skidmore College.

The shift occurred first in New York, at Grand Central, on Sunday, November 18, which became known as the Day of Two Noons. Tampering with time alarmed some New Yorkers with what would have been Y2K trepidation, but most cheerfully anticipated the shift that advanced midday to 3 minutes, 58 seconds, and 38 hundredths of a second earlier than it had been the day before. In room 48 of the Western Union Building at 195 Broadway, James Hamblet signaled the new noon by dropping the official 42-inch-wide, 125-pound cooper ball from a 22-foot-high staff poised on the roof for navigators and jewelers to see. (To accommodate the New York Central's Sunday-morning schedule, Hamblet had actually stopped the pendulum of his official regulator clock first at 9:00 A.M.)

"There was no convulsion of nature," the *New-York Tribune* dryly noted, "and no signs have been discovered of political or social revolution." Time marched on after a brief halt, and all was right with the world, or at least with the railroads. Five years after Grand Central opened in 1913, Congress imposed Daylight Saving Time and standardized the time zones during World War I. Reverend Dowd lived to see his proposal adopted by the railroads but not by the government. In 1904 he was struck by a train at a grade crossing in upstate New York. No record survives of whether the train was on time.

·40·

The Stoop

Stepping Out

The outside steps of row houses became a distinctive feature of New York City street life only in the nineteenth century, although the stoop was introduced long before by the Dutch (the word means "small platform" or "staircase").

"The high entrance steps," Mario Maffi wrote in *New York City: An Outsider's Inside View,* "almost give the old New York houses the appearance of small castles." He suggests that they were inspired by Dutch buildings, elevated to evade North Sea floods and flush with the street to compensate for space consumed by canals in cities like Amsterdam.

The stoop was a fixture in Elmer Rice's play *Street Scene,* was depicted in *The Godfather; Part II,* and even survived into television series from *Sesame Street* to *The Wire* ("stoop kids" in Baltimore were supervised by their parents, while "corner kids" were not).

Most town houses in the city were originally built with stoops. They led up to the family's private living quarters, which included the parlor and dining room, with the kitchen and service areas accessible from an entrance at street level or below, in what became known as the "English basement" plan. In the twentieth century, many of the graceful and imposing staircases anchoring brownstones were removed as owners divided grand single-family homes into rental apartments.

"The row house with stoop prevailed in New York until the turn of this century, when the concept of living in multiple dwellings began to gain wide acceptance," says Regina M. Kellerman, a historic preservationist.

Now many owners who lost their stoops want them back. "If you can afford to buy a single-family row house now in Manhattan," said Andrew S. Dolkart, director of Columbia University's historic preservation program, "you can usually afford to put the stoop back."

The stoop figured prominently in Jane Jacobs's *The Death and Life of Great American Cities* as a vital component of energizing street life—"the ballet of the good city sidewalk"—which, in turn, was invigorated by it. "The sidewalk must have users on it fairly continuously, both to add to the number of effective eyes on the street and to induce the people in buildings along the street to watch the sidewalks in sufficient numbers. Nobody enjoys sitting on a stoop or looking out a window on an empty street," Jacobs wrote (which is why the old popular song "The Sidewalks of New York" was the city's unofficial anthem for decades).

Stoops contributed to a culture of gatherings and games (remember stoop-ball?) and served as ad hoc community centers in many neighborhoods where New Yorkers were, as one reader recalled, "sitting out in the evening talking with neighbors, watching their kids play, taking relief from the heat." Those practices have revived in Brownstone Brooklyn and similar neighborhoods.

·41·

The Critic

How the Other Half Lived

A *Tale of Two Cities* had little to do with the poverty Charles Dickens witnessed two decades earlier on his tour of the Five Points slums in 1842, but the title has become a metaphor for income inequality anyway. (Benjamin Disraeli's "two nations" would have been more apt.) Bill de Blasio invoked the phrase in his successful 2013 New York mayoral campaign, having borrowed it from Fernando Ferrer, the former Bronx borough president, who used it eight years earlier and who acknowledged: "I stole it from Mario Cuomo, who stole it from R.F.K., who stole it from Michael Harrington, who stole it from Jacob Riis, who stole it from Dickens, et cetera. By now it should be public domain."

The theme has been universal—and recurring—because the income gap has never gone away. In 2012 the richest fifth of Manhattanites made over forty times what the lowest fifth reported ($391,000 versus $9,600).

The gap is graphically revealed in what is arguably Weegee's most enduring image, his November 22, 1943, staged photograph dubbed *The Critic*. It features the withering expression of an inebriated woman imported from a Bowery dive as she sizes up two socialites (Mrs. George Washington Kavenaugh and Lady Decies) arriving for the Metropolitan Opera's opening night at the old yellow-brick house on Broadway and West Thirty-Ninth Street. The eviscerating visage captured New York's cultural and economic divide, which survived the evolution of the alms houses to welfare and food stamps and today has reached proportions that some politicians, public officials, and advocates for the poor describe as an inequality crisis.

Weegee (the photographer Arthur Fellig; the name was a corruption of "Ouija," a nickname inspired by Fellig's timely, telepathic arrival at crime scenes) vividly captured the juxtaposition. Years later, Robert Walker captured a similar dichotomy in a classic photograph that depicted two contrasting limbs protruding from

a midtown taxi—the driver's hairy arm and a woman thrusting a cigarette holder from the back window. (The only anachronism in this contrasting view might be the cigarette.)

Deriding the elitist nineteenth-century notion that only four hundred pluto-crats really counted in New York City, O. Henry credited "a wiser man"—the census taker—with a "larger estimate of human interest," which he memorialized in fiction as *The Four Million.* The four hundred (supposedly the number who could fit in Mrs. Astor's ballroom) stuck, though. Nothing epitomized the excesses of that age, or its last gasp, more than the Bradley-Martin ball on February 10, 1897. Cornelia Bradley-Martin lowered the bar enough to let eight hundred aristocrats participate in what was dubbed "the greatest party in the history of the city," a multimillion-dollar costume fete (it cost the hosts almost $9 million in today's dollars) that transformed the old Waldorf-Astoria Hotel into a replica of Versailles and redefined wretched excess. Bradley Martin (his wife hyphenated his name) may have begun with a noble goal: to give a concert that might help lift the spirits of a city mired in a depression. His wife had a better idea: a costume party on short notice, so guests would have to patronize local merchants rather than import their attire from Paris. She came as Mary, Queen of Scots, he as Louis XV (about fifty women, apparently oblivious to the consequences of her "Let them eat cake" advice, appeared as Marie Antoinette).

A few days later, the Reverend George L. Perlin delivered a sermon at his Every-Day Church that echoed the sentiments of a chorus of clergymen and civic leaders. He said the ball "involved a great waste, notwithstanding the familiar excuses that are made for it, even by so-called philanthropists, on the ground that it benefits the poor. If the enormous sum—$100,000 or $200,000, whatever it may have been, did accomplish good, it was not intentionally expended with that object in view, but solely to provide an evening's entertainment for a limited number of people." After what was called the last hurrah of the Gilded Age, the Bradley-Martins were more or less laughed out of town. They decamped for their second home in Britain and returned to New York only once.

· 42 ·

Civic Fame

The Face of the City

She is three times larger than life and gilded, which is what you would expect, and her back faces Brooklyn, which is not particularly surprising, either. Audrey Munson, the model after whom she was sculpted, once appeared naked in a porn film (she of the face that launched a thousand quips, she listed herself in a city directory first as an actress, then as an artist) and later was declared insane. All in all, a fitting physical manifestation of the prescient, if decidedly uneasy, consolidation in 1898 of what would become Greater New York. ("Greater" is a geographic term; the City Charter refers only to the City of New York.)

The five boroughs are now home to 8.4 million people, but if New Yorkers had not overcome considerable ambivalence, Los Angeles might be the nation's largest city (with 3.8 million), followed by Chicago (2.7 million) and Brooklyn (2.5 million). Manhattan—the original New York, with 1.7 million—would rank fifth or sixth, behind Houston and, perhaps, Queens.

The bumpy road to consolidation was smoothed earlier in the nineteenth century by the plodding but inevitable imposition of the Manhattan street grid and, later, the opening of the Brooklyn Bridge. In 1898, Manhattan—the City of New York—merged with the eastern Bronx (the western portion had been annexed in

1874), western Queens County (a year later the county fractured as three towns formed Nassau County), Kings County (Brooklyn) and Staten Island. Westchester demurred. Inauguration of subway service in 1904, followed by construction of arterial highways and additional spans across the East and Harlem Rivers in the twentieth century, welded the tenuous legal framework of conglomeration of the five disparate boroughs into a concrete and cultural reality.

Again not surprisingly, the most visible symbols of consolidation can be seen in Manhattan (Brooklyn's 1894 referendum to relinquish its status as a city and jeopardize its Protestant homogeneity passed by a suspect 277 votes of 129,000 cast). There's Albert Weinert's allegorical marble frieze in the Surrogate's Court building, which depicts a youth, symbolizing the new city, flanked by Miss Brooklyn reaching out to Miss New York. But the most visible representation is across the street, atop McKim, Mead & White's beaux arts 580-foot-high Municipal Building. She is called *Civic Fame.* The twenty-five-foot-tall statue by Adolph A. Weinman, who also worked on Pennsylvania Station and the Prison Ship Martyrs' Monument, was installed in 1913 at a cost of nine thousand dollars. Standing heroically on a globe, she is described as the city's highest statue and the third largest, after the Statue of Liberty and Jacques Lipchitz's *Bellerophon Taming Pegasus* on Columbia Law School's facade.

Like the Statue of Liberty, the 985-square-foot figure, which weighs 2,500 pounds, is fashioned from hammered copper on an iron frame. Barefoot, she holds a shield with the city's coat of arms (it plunged through a skylight in 1936 but was restored) and a laurel branch in her right hand and a mural crown crenelated by five turrets, symbolizing the five boroughs, in her left. Dolphins represent the city's maritime heritage.

In her eighth decade and suffering from exposure, the statue was removed, restored, and regilded with hand-burnished 23.5-karat gold leaf, and hoisted back into position by helicopter in 1991. That was only four years before Audrey Munson died in an upstate asylum, just short of her 105th birthday. Munson's placid but purposeful face is everywhere, guarding the Maine monument near Columbus Circle and leading General Sherman in Grand Army Plaza. "If the name of Miss Manhattan belongs to anyone in particular," the *New York Sun* wrote, "it is to this young woman."

·43·

The Bagel

A Whole in One

The first known mention of the bagel dates from 1610, in the community regulations of Krakow, Poland. Today the world's biggest bagel factory may be in Illinois. Still, no other food is so associated with New York as the "Jewish English muffin," which spread from the Lower East Side in the early twentieth century.

What is a bagel? Ed Levine offered this mouthwatering description in *The New York Times*: "A round bread made of simple, elegant ingredients: high-gluten flour, salt, water, yeast, and malt. Its dough is boiled, then baked, and the result should be a rich caramel color; it should not be pale and blond. A bagel should weigh four ounces or less and should make a slight cracking sound when you bite into it instead of a whoosh. A bagel should be eaten warm and, ideally, should be no more than four or five hours old when consumed. All else is not a bagel."

Theories abound about the bagel's origin. In her book *The Bagel*, Maria Balinska offers several versions, including the possibility that they migrated from Germany to Poland during the fourteenth century (a variant of doughy pretzels made in monasteries for feast days) and that they transmogrified into round rolls with holes, called *obwarzanek* (Jews in Poland were granted the right to bake bread, a foodstuff normally associated with church rituals, only in the late thirteenth cen-

tury.) Another theory credits the bagel to a Viennese baker who, honoring King Jan Sobieski of Poland, a horse lover, shaped his doughy offering like a *beugel*—German for stirrup.

By the1990s, columnist William Safire wrote in the *Times,* "a sea change in American taste" had taken place: "The bagel overtook the doughnut in popularity. Today we spend three-quarters of a billion dollars a year on bagels, only a half-billion on doughnuts." But he and others lamented the loss of the old artistry as bagels were mass-produced by machines, which took over the former hand rolling. Less-time-consuming steaming was substituted for boiling. Steel ovens replaced stone. "The formerly chewy morsel that once had to be separated from the rest of its ring by a sharp jerk of the eater's head is now devoid of character—half-baked, seeking to be all pastry to all men," Safire wrote.

Even though bagels are ubiquitous today, they are still associated with the city where they thrived in the twentieth century more than anyplace else. "Pizza belongs to America now," said Josh Ozersky, a food writer, "but the bagel was always the undisputed property of New York."

·44·

General Slocum

Opening Hell's Gate

Terrible affair that General Slocum explosion," James Joyce wrote in *Ulysses*, which took place entirely the day after the *Slocum* disaster. "Terrible, terrible. A thousand casualties. And heartrending scenes. Men trampling down women and children. Most brutal thing. What do they say was the cause? Spontaneous combustion. Most scandalous revelation. Not a single lifeboat would float and the fire hose all burst. What I can't understand is how the inspectors ever allowed a boat like that. . . ."

Few natural disasters have altered the face of New York in recorded history, but some man-made catastrophes have—none more so than the sinking of the coal-fired excursion steamboat *General Slocum* in 1904.

The 235-foot-long wooden side-wheeler, built in Brooklyn in 1891 and named for a Civil War general and New York congressman, had been chartered for Wednesday, June 15, by St. Mark's Evangelical Lutheran Church in Kleindeutschland, or Little Germany, which flanked Tompkins Square on the Lower East Side of Manhattan. German immigrants are sometimes overlooked in the influx of Irish, Italians, and Eastern European Jews, but as early as the mid-nineteenth century, New York was home to more German-speakers than any other city except Berlin and Vienna.

As she was steaming up the East River near Ninetieth Street at about 9:30 A.M. to a church picnic at Eatons Neck on Long Island with about thirteen hundred passengers, mostly women and children, the *General Slocum* caught fire. Whatever the cause, oily rags and fuel fed the flames. By the time the boat sank off North Brother Island, more than a thousand people had died, either in the fire or in the water. Funerals went on for a week. One of the victims was three-year-old Anna Liebenow, whose body was recovered several days later. Her black leather shoes were kept by her sister, Adella, who was among the 321 known survivors, who mostly clung to rotted life preservers or swam to shore.

Of the eight people indicted by a federal grand jury, only the captain was convicted and only for criminal negligence. He served three and a half years of a ten-year sentence. Subsequent regulations improved passenger safety, and women (including Gertrude Ederle, who would become an Olympic champion and the first woman to swim the English Channel) were taught to swim. Little Germany was devastated by the disaster—the city's worst until 9/11 and its worst maritime accident ever. Most of its Lutheran German residents moved uptown to Yorkville and elsewhere to escape the memory. The tragedy was marked by a memorial at Lutheran All Faiths Cemetery in Middle Village, Queens, and by a marble fountain in Tompkins Square Park, which carries the inscription "They are Earth's purest children, young and fair." The last surviving passenger died in 2004. She was six months old when the *General Slocum* sank. Her two elder sisters—one was Anna Liebenow—died in the accident.

·45·

Dreamland Bell

The Last Resort

I was walking again in Dreamland," Henry Miller wrote in *Tropic of Capricorn*, "and a man was walking above me on a tightrope and above him a man was sitting in an airplane spelling letters of smoke in the sky."

After May 27, 1911, young men could no longer invite young ladies to "Meet Me Tonight at Dreamland"—not the Coney Island version in Brooklyn, anyway. The famous amusement park burned to a crisp in a spectacular fire that started when some of the park's million electric lightbulbs began to explode. One plunged into a bucket of hot tar spilled in the dark by a workman caulking a leak in the Hell Gate water ride just a few hours before the opening on Memorial Day weekend of what would have been its eighth season. By dawn, all fifteen acres of Dreamland were completely destroyed.

Coney Island was aptly named by prescient Indian sun-worshippers as "Place Without Shadows" and rechristened by the Dutch for the rabbits (coneys) that proliferated there. Coney was "Sodom by the Sea," an egalitarian sand spit at the bottom of Brooklyn (now attached to the borough by landfill) that drew millions of New Yorkers and visitors to amusement parks, hot dog and seafood emporia, and the Boardwalk (the name is becoming anachronistic, as the lumber is being

replaced with concrete). Since the mid-nineteenth century, they came mostly by rail from other parts of Brooklyn and by a two-hour steam ferry from Manhattan.

In addition to Hell Gate, Dreamland featured a Lilliputian Village inhabited by three hundred dwarfs, a firefighting demonstration, an incubator for premature babies, and a one-armed lion tamer, but it faced tough competition from neighboring Steeplechase and Luna Park, which opened in 1897 and 1903, respectively.

Dreamland was the nonpartisan brainchild of Brooklyn and Manhattan political bosses. The park employed 14,000 people and could easily accommodate 100,000 visitors simultaneously.

Steeplechase, Rem Koolhaas wrote, was "where the park format is invented almost by accident under the pressure of a hysterical demand for entertainment; Luna, where this format is invested with thematic and architectural coherence; and finally Dreamland, where the preceding breakthroughs are elevated to an ideological plane by a professional politician . . . a post-proletarian park."

When Steeplechase suffered a fire in 1907, its canny proprietor, George C. Tilyou, turned it into an opportunity. He posted a sign outside that read: "I have troubles today that I had not yesterday I had troubles yesterday that I have not today." Then he promised to build a bigger, better amusement park. Meanwhile, he charged gawkers ten cents to tour the ruins.

Steeplechase (with its giant Ferris wheel and mechanical horse racecourse and, after the 1939 World's Fair in New York, the 270-foot tall Parachute Jump) would survive until 1964, the last of the old amusement parks to close in Brooklyn's last resort. Dreamland would not be rebuilt. It's now the site of the New York Aquarium. The only major Dreamland artifact to survive was a five-hundred-pound bronze bell that announced the arrival of boats at the twelve-hundred-foot-long New Iron Pier. ("They cannot burn! They cannot sink!" the Iron Steamboat Co. proclaimed only a few years after the *General Slocum* tragedy.)

The bell was discovered a hundred yards offshore and retrieved in 2009 by Gene Ritter, a professional diver from Brooklyn.

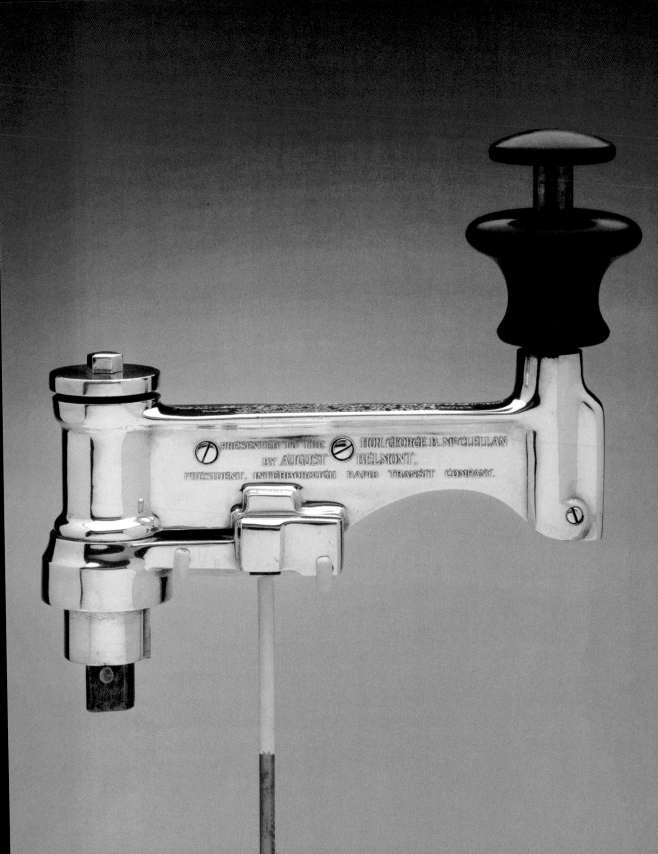

·46·

Subway Throttle

A Switch in Time

At 2:35 P.M. on Thursday, October 27, 1904, Mayor George B. McClellan, Jr., son of the Civil War general, was supposed to pose for pictures with his hand on the Tiffany sterling silver, steel, and ebony throttle. However, no mere photo op would suffice for McClellan. "I'm running this train," he declared, and drove the olive green subway cars on their maiden trip all the way to West 103rd Street—even skipping some local stops (the trip took twenty-two minutes; returning as a local from 145th Street, the train was ten minutes late). An estimated 150,000 passengers bought nickel tickets that day and boarded the subway between 7:00 P.M., when it opened to the public, and midnight. (The first reported theft was of a five-hundred-dollar diamond horseshoe pin that day belonging to Henry Barrett of 348 West Forty-Sixth Street.)

The Interborough Rapid Transit Company operated the original 9.1-mile long subway line that consisted of twenty-eight stations beginning at City Hall (it veered west at Grand Central to accommodate, and facilitate, the booming Times Square). IRT service expanded to the Bronx two years later, to Brooklyn in 1908, and to Queens in 1915. McClellan, accompanied by Archbishop John M. Farley and perhaps most remembered for canceling all movie theater licenses (he claimed celluloid film was a fire hazard and the films themselves were a moral hazard), declared before his audacious drive that "without rapid transit Greater New York would be little more than a geographical expression." By the time he returned to City Hall, *The New York Times* reported, "the mayor was smoking a cigar which looked guiltily short, as if he had lighted it on the train."

"For the first time in his life Father Knickerbocker went underground," the paper reported, "he and his children, to the number of 150,000, amid the tooting of whistles and the firing of salutes, for a first ride in a subway which for years had been scoffed at as an impossibility." The article already detected different demeanors among riders: "The up-bound Brooklynites and Jerseyites and Richmondites had boarded the trains with the stolid air of an African chief suddenly admitted into civilization and unwilling to admit that anything surprised him. The Manhattanites boarded the trains with the sneaking air of men who were ashamed to admit that they were doing something new, and attempting to cover up the disgraceful fact."

The subway wove its way into the city's cultural fabric with Duke Ellington's "Take the A Train," the chase scene from *The French Connection,* and baseball's Subway Series. The system now has 468 stations, the most of any in the world, serving 26 lines, the longest of which is the A train, stretching 32 miles from the northern tip of Manhattan to southeastern Queens. Some 6,300 cars operate on 659 miles of track. New York's subway is one of the few rapid transit systems that are open 24/7. Today weekday ridership tops 7.6 million for an annual total of 2.3 billion, or nearly six times the population of the United States.

·47·

Black-and-White Cookie

We Are What We Eat

Leave the gun," Richard Castellano, as Peter Clemenza, the loyal Corleone capo, orders his henchman after rubbing out a turncoat in a parked car in the 1972 film *The Godfather*. Then the Bronx-born Castellano memorably ad-libs: "Take the cannoli."

You don't have to be a Mob capo to savor a fresh cannoli or, for that matter, to deserve your just desserts. No subject engaged *Times* readers who contributed to our original objects list more than food did. They weighed in passionately for pizza, egg creams, Mello-Rolls, Ebinger's blackout cake, and more.

We couldn't include them all—this isn't a cookbook—so we exercised literary license and chose my favorite, which many New Yorkers embraced, too: the black-and-white cookie. It barely qualifies as a cookie; it's more like a cake. It's not even black (the icing is chocolate brown). Somehow, though, it democratically says New York (from subway bakeries to shrink-wrapped varieties in bodegas and delis,

to William Greenberg Desserts and Eleven Madison Park, where the tasting menu is $195 per person, cookie included).

Who baked the first black-and-white? The cookie's provenance is sketchy. Some experts trace it to Hemstrought's Bakery in upstate Utica, New York, about a century ago, but those often had a fluffier chocolate base and fudge frosting, although vanilla versions were sold, too. In some locales (upstate New York and New England) they are called half-moons or harlequins, though black-and-whites are generally bigger and topped with a fondant frosting. Germany boasts a version known generically as Amerikaner.

During his 2008 presidential campaign, Barack Obama visited a delicatessen in Fort Lauderdale, Florida, where he dubbed them Unity Cookies. The black-and-white also was invoked in a *Seinfeld* episode as a metaphor for racial harmony and peace between the sexes, specifically George and Elaine ("Look to the cookie!" Jerry declares in a crowded bakery). Jerry Seinfeld notwithstanding, no real New Yorker eats a black-and-white cookie down the middle. You reveal a lot about yourself depending on whether you save the chocolate or the vanilla half for last.

"Unlike other edible icons, like New York cheesecake or bagels, there is no such thing as a delicious black-and-white cookie—they are either edible or inedible," Molly O'Neill wrote in *The New York Times*. "They are the runes of deli counters and bakeries. Why? Because they are not what they appear to be. Black-and-white cookies are not even cookies. They are floury cakes baked in a cookie style. They are broken promises. They are irony with kitsch. Seinfeld was right. If you look to the cookie, you get New York."

•48•

Battle's Badge

A Hue and Cry over Blurring the Blue Line

Acentury ago, blacks on the New York City Police Department force constituted a minority of one. Samuel Battle moved to New York for good in 1901, when the city's sixty thousand or so blacks accounted for under 2 percent of the population. He worked as a houseboy at a hotel and as a Red Cap at Grand Central Terminal. A decade later, he became the first black man appointed to the New York City police force. Battle, who was sworn in in 1911, went on to become the first black sergeant and the first black lieutenant as well.

The intersection of race and crime was being hotly debated then, too. In recounting his career for the Harlem Renaissance poet Langston Hughes, as revealed in a forthcoming book by Arthur Browne, Battle recalled: "During the summer of 1911 sightseers in buses and old-fashioned autos such as Stanley Steamers, Stutz, Packards and Rolls-Royces came from different parts of the city and out of town to stare at me as one of the sights of New York. Every time I stood on a corner crowds gathered. Automobiles, horse-drawn cabs and passing drays got in each other's way while the riders gazed at me. Motormen clanged their bells and brought their trolleys to a full stop as conductors pointed me out to curious passengers. I was the first Negro policeman in the history of Manhattan Island. So much fuss had never been made over me before in my life. Meanwhile, I stood straight as an arrow, perspired with dignity, and tried not to notice the excitement. I was both embarrassed and amused. It may sound like an exaggeration to say that once the mere combination of a brown skin with the blue uniform of New York's Finest caused a traffic jam. It is no exaggeration."

He reported for duty at 7:00 A.M. at the old Twenty-Eighth Precinct Station on West Sixty-Eight Street: "The men listed for my shift were gathering in the back room as I came in. I said 'Good morning' as I entered. You could have cut the silence with a knife. While we were waiting to receive our group instructions from the sergeant, some of the men talked among themselves. Nobody said a word to me."

A crowd was waiting when he emerged from the station house. "Standing inspection for the first time, I did not even bat an eye as the sun shone on my shiny new badge, number 782."

By 2010, for the first time, non-Hispanic whites accounted for a minority of rank-and-file New York police officers, about two decades after the city's overall population had passed that benchmark. Among the more than 22,000 cops on patrol, 53 percent were black, Hispanic, or Asian (while Benjamin Ward, the city's first black police commissioner, was appointed as far back as 1983). The proportion of sergeants, lieutenants, and captains was 43 percent, 29 percent, and 21 percent, respectively. It took a while for Battle to work his way into the hearts of fellow officers. He finally won them over in 1919, when he rescued a white officer from a crowd of rioters in Harlem. "The white officers worked in an all-Negro neighborhood, practically," Battle recalled, "and they needed me as much as I needed them and sometimes more."

·49·

Triangle Monument

The Birth of the New Deal

Until as recently as 2010, some of the victims still remained unidentified. The Triangle shirtwaist factory fire in 1911 claimed 146 lives, mostly young immigrant workers at the factory, on Washington Place and Greene Street in Manhattan, where exits were locked or blocked. (The building still stands and now houses New York University classrooms.) The legacy of the tragedy is reflected in tougher fire codes, the ascent of organized labor, and the beginnings of the New Deal.

Most of the victims were unglorified (a monument to the six recently identified was erected at the Cemetery of the Evergreens on the border of Brooklyn and Queens), but the Triangle fire propelled other individuals to greater prominence. Among them was Max D. Steuer, the premier defense lawyer of his day, who defended the factory owners. He gingerly asked a young garment worker to repeat her word-for-word eyewitness testimony, suggesting that it might have been rehearsed and memorized. On the fourth account, he interrupted her:

"Katie, have you not forgotten a word?"

"Yes, sir," she replied, smiling. "I left out one word."

"Well, tell the story again and put the word in," Steuer said.

She did. The two owners were acquitted.

IN SYMPATHY AND SORROW
CITIZENS OF NEW YORK
RAISE THIS MONUMENT
OVER THE GRAVES OF
UNIDENTIFIED WOMEN AND
CHILDREN WHO WITH ONE
HUNDRED AND THIRTY NINE
OTHERS PERISHED BY FIRE IN
THE TRIANGLE SHIRTWAIST
FACTORY WASHINGTON PLACE
MARCH 25 1911

Rose Schneiderman, the eldest daughter of a tailor, was the conscience of the labor movement. Her message at an April 2, 1911, memorial service for the Triangle fire victims at the Metropolitan Opera House riveted the public. "I would be a traitor to those poor burned bodies if I came here to talk good fellowship," she declared. "Too much blood has been spilled. I know from my experience it is up to the working people to save themselves. The only way they can save themselves is by a strong working-class movement."

Anne Morgan, the youngest daughter of the financier J. Pierpont Morgan, was another transformative figure, instrumental in recruiting socialites to the cause of workingwomen. (She was also a pioneer in transforming the hangout of the Dead End Kids into Sutton Place; her town house is now home to the United Nations secretary-general.)

Two Democratic clubhouse politicians from Manhattan, Assemblyman Alfred E. Smith and Senator Robert F. Wagner, led a Factory Investigation Commission, which expanded its mandate to include child labor, minimum wages, and sanitary conditions. Smith represented the Lower East Side, where many Triangle victims lived. He was a Tammany Hall stalwart, and to give credit where it is due, elevating worker safety to the state agenda would have required the approval of the local Democratic leader, Timothy D. Sullivan, known as Big Tim, and Charles F. Murphy, the sagacious boss of Tammany Hall. They valued the lives of their constituents as well as their votes. Smith was elected governor in 1918 and was the unsuccessful Democratic nominee for president in 1928.

Frances Perkins, commission member, was a thirty-year-old Boston-born social worker who would become Franklin Roosevelt's secretary of labor. She was visiting a friend on the opposite side of Washington Square Park that Saturday, March 25, 1911, when they heard sirens and screams and rushed to the scene. Perkins, the executive secretary of the National Consumers League and a lobbyist for the fire-inspired Committee on Safety, galvanized New York's officials. "The Triangle fire was a torch that lighted up the whole industrial scene," Perkins said. She would describe the Triangle fire as "the day the New Deal began."

·50·

The Automat

The Origin of Fast Food

Audrey Meadows worked there in *That Touch of Mink.* Marlo Thomas met a photographer there in an episode of *That Girl.* Joan Crawford longs for a fellow patron's dessert in *Sadie McKee.* In *Easy Living,* Jean Arthur calmly digests her beef potpie while cafeteria chaos ensues. Neeley ate there in *A Tree Grows in Brooklyn.* An Irving Berlin ditty evokes the place ("Let's have another cup of coffee"), as do the lyrics of *Gentlemen Prefer Blondes.* The advertising slogan "Less work for Mother" became a middle-class mantra for retail take-home food.

Until industrialization in the nineteenth century, a leisurely lunch was called dinner and typically was consumed at home. The proliferation of blue-collar and white-collar workers transformed dinner into the lunch hour (or half hour). No innovation hastened that transformation more than the fast-food conceit that Joseph Horn and Frank Hardart borrowed from Europe. The Automat, launched in Philadelphia, opened in Times Square on July 2, 1912, and the concept eventually replaced the so-called free lunch at saloons shuttered by Prohibition.

It was cheap, egalitarian (open seating, no anti-democratic tipping that validated class distinctions, no smoking), and elegant. Chrome and brass vending machines framed by Italian marble conveyed cleanliness, because the workers who prepared the food were invisible behind the spinning steel drums that fed the automatic dispensers. Patrons could choose exactly which piece of pie or crock of baked beans they preferred (all of the dishes were prepared at a commissary on Eleventh Avenue). With no cash registers, customers rarely computed the total cost of several courses as they inserted nickels in each slot, opening a glass door to retrieve their food or beverage.

The average man becomes a "manipulator of destiny," suddenly finding himself "before Ali Baba's cave," an Australian observer wrote. "He whispers, 'Open sesame!' and lo! a ham sandwich or a peach dumpling is his for the taking, also for a nickel."

Even as homeless people began congregating at Automats (Edward Hopper's famous 1927 painting of a lone woman at a cafeteria was titled *Automat*), customers were typically allowed to linger over a half-full cup of coffee or homemade lemonade (free water and a lemon) or tomato soup (hot water with ketchup). But the Automats fell victim to even faster-food joints and the limits of their own technology, the patented mechanical dispensers that accepted only nickels and quarters. Dolphin-shaped spigots dispensed coffee, but by the early 1950s, the company was losing a few cents on every nickel cup sold. The last Automat, at East Forty-Second Street and Third Avenue, closed in 1991.

The playwright Neil Simon recalled that he learned more from his dining partners there than during three years at Princeton: "And the years went by and I turned from a day customer to a night patron, working on those first attempts at monologues and sketches at two in the morning, over steaming black coffee and fresh cheese Danish. And a voice from the stranger opposite me.

"'Where you from? California?'

"'No. I grew up in New York.'

"'Is that so? Where in New York?'

"'At this table.'"

·51·

Armory Show

"Cultural Sabotage"

Who knew that even New Yorkers could be shocked? But a 1913 art exhibit did just that. The eye-popping one-month show was billed modestly as an International Exhibition of Modern Art, but the exhibit at the Sixty-Ninth Regiment Armory on Lexington Avenue and East Twenty-Sixth Street proved nothing short of revolutionary. Pioneering and experimental post-impressionistic, cubist, fauvist, and futuristic styles defied conventional realism and prevailing views of what constituted art.

What became known universally as *the* Armory Show introduced about 1,300 works of 300 avant-garde artists, including Mary Cassatt (her brother, Alexander, was president of the Pennsylvania Railroad and had just built the neoclassical Penn Station), Cézanne, Degas, Hassam, Kandinsky, Matisse, Monet, Picasso, Seurat, and Toulouse-Lautrec to American audiences.

The New York of 1913, Holland Cotter wrote a century later in *The New York Times,* was not yet the world cultural capital. Rather, it was a "seething, manic place with a powerful but provincial population," challenging London's preeminence as global economic capital, topping out the planet's tallest skyscraper, the Woolworth Building, and reverberating with demands from women for the right to vote and millworkers to organize and earn a decent living.

"At one time, a New Yorker rattled by noise and change could seek solace in art, in the visual smoothness and moral sureties of, say, Gilded Age painting, with its lush landscapes, classical tableaus and teatime interiors. Now, suddenly, that option was being all but closed," Cotter wrote. He described the Armory Show as a deliberate "act of cultural sabotage." It was designed to shock, and it did. Marcel Duchamp's cubist *Nude Descending a Staircase* prompted one critic to compare it to "an explosion in a shingle factory" and a parodist in the *New York Evening Sun* to depict "The Rude Descending a Staircase," which satirized rush-hour straphangers in the subway.

One of the organizers, Walt Kuhn, drew on his promotional skills, papering the city with posters and campaign buttons (a precursor of the Metropolitan Museum of Art's admission buttons) festooned with a logo featuring an uprooted Revolutionary War–style liberty tree.

Theodore Roosevelt, considered a moderate in his criticism, described the artists as "extremists" and attributed to them "the powers to make folly lucrative which the late P. T. Barnum showed with his faked mermaid. There are thousands of people who will pay small sums to look at a faked mermaid; and now and then one of this kind with enough money will buy a Cubist picture, or a picture of a misshapen nude woman, repellent from every standpoint."

The show (which subsequently traveled to Chicago and Boston) had the desired effect: for American artists, it was a catalyst. Spectators were scandalized, captivated, and confused—a reaction captured by the quizzical couple depicted in a 1998 postage stamp.

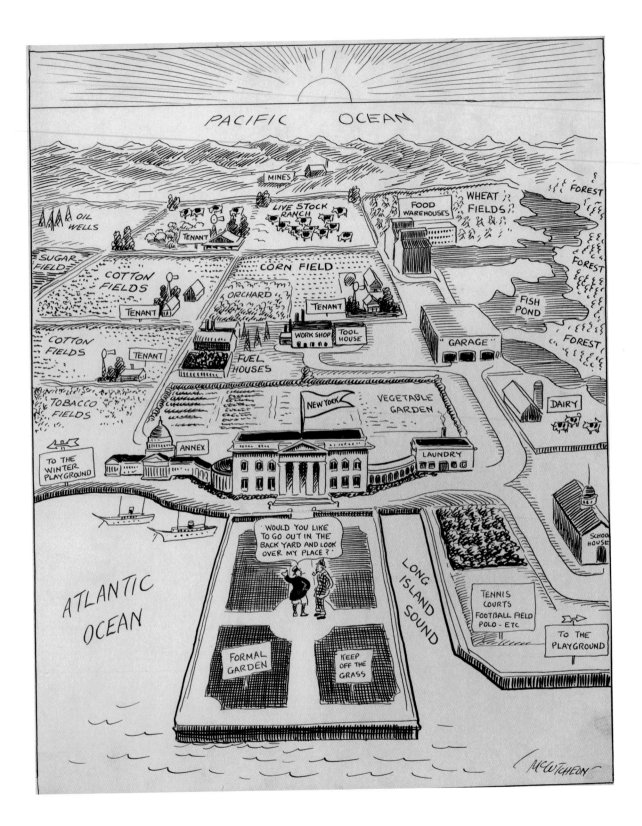

·52·

New Yorkers' View

Cockeyed Optimists

Published views of New York date from 1651, and most have been embellished with a liberal dose of artistic license. Not for nothing did Russell Shorto proclaim early New Amsterdam as "the island at the center of the world."

Perhaps the most famous representation of New York's smug myopic world-view was Saul Steinberg's 1976 *New Yorker* cover illustration. It relegated the rest of the United States, between the Hudson River and the Pacific Ocean, to a non-descript avenue-wide sliver on the horizon. New Yorkers needed a robust display of boosterism back then. Only the year before, the city was tottering on the precipice of financial default. But 1976 marked a brief respite, as rampant crime and turmoil were subsumed by the nation's ebullient bicentennial celebration and the Democratic National Convention.

Steinberg's ironic ink, pencil, and watercolor drawing, titled *View of the World from Ninth Avenue,* captured New York chauvinism at its most vulnerable. It also inspired myriad imitators. Less known is that it was itself preceded by three centuries of self-aggrandizing panoramas. Even Johannes Vingboons's 1665 depiction of New Amsterdam was an idealized view crafted, in part, as a tourist poster for the fledgling colony. Later bird's-eye views, like John Bachmann's in 1859, provided a parabolic prism that overstated the city's centrality.

In the twentieth century, two other, more obscure visions provided insights into New Yorkers' self-indulgence. Both were published during the Roaring Twenties, when the popular perception of the cosmopolis generously reflected and contributed to intemperance. In 1928, Daniel K. Wallingford of Boston, after what he described as "patient research," published his *New Yorker's Idea of the United States of America*. Long Island was bigger than Texas. Manhattan was nearly as long as California. Even Staten Island was larger than West Virginia. Cape Cod, Hollywood, and Florida were each outsized. Wallingford quoted average citizens of this "nation within a nation": "We have cousins in the West. They live in Wilmington, Del." "He is moving to Dallas so he can be near his little mother in El Paso."

Six years earlier, John T. McCutcheon, an Indianan, drew his *New Yorker's Idea of the Map of the United States* for the *Chicago Tribune*. The centerpiece was a building resembling the White House but emblazoned with a "New York" banner (the Capitol was off to one side, labeled "Annex"; on the other side was a "laundry," possibly to clean perpetually dirty linen). One critic later described the map's lopsided geography as "an uncanny anticipation" of Steinberg's celebrated magazine cover.

"The New Yorker's garage is, appropriately, placed in the general vicinity of Detroit, and New England contains his school house," according to a curator's description of McCutcheon's oeuvre.

"The vast acreage devoted to agriculture, mining, forestry and oil wells suggests a colonial empire feeding the pleasures of the great metropolis, personified by"—what else?—"a knickerbocker-clad playboy at its center."

·53·

Baseball Card

How Gehrig's Streak Began

A record crowd of more than 74,200 fans—the biggest in baseball history up to that time—turned out on April 18, 1923, to celebrate the opening of Yankee Stadium in the Bronx. An additional 25,000 were turned away. The commissioner of baseball came by subway.

The fifteen-cent opening day "souvenir programme" featured Colonel Jacob Ruppert, the Yankees' owner, on the cover (the publisher was listed as Harry M. Stevens, whose firm would go on to sell millions of peanuts and Cracker Jack boxes). John Philip Sousa led the Seventh Regiment Band. Governor Alfred E. Smith defied the typical opening-day program by throwing the first pitch flawlessly. In the third inning, Babe Ruth redeemed his disappointing 1922 season by delivering a decisive homer into the bleachers. Initiating a tradition that defined the Bronx and continues today, the Yankees beat the Red Sox, 4 to 1.

Playing first base that season was thirty-year-old Chicago-born Walter Clement Pipp, who had been with the team since 1915 (he started with Detroit one season, 1913), led the American League with 12 home runs in 1916 and 9 in 1917, and in 569 at-bats in 1923 would average .304. (Pipp's fielding average in 1923 was an impressive .992.)

Pipp batted left-handed, like his backup, a kid from Columbia University

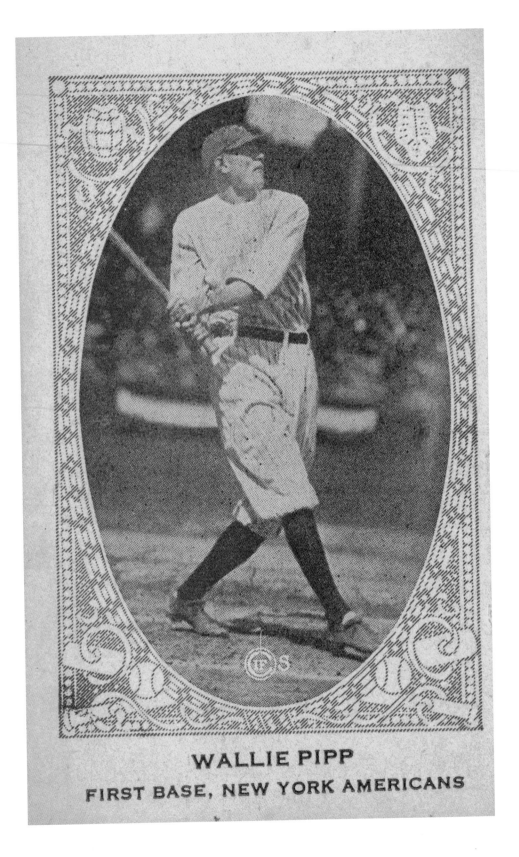

WALLIE PIPP

FIRST BASE, NEW YORK AMERICANS

whom he had scouted and recommended to manager Miller Huggins. The kid, who filled in at first base on June 15, four days shy of turning twenty, was Lou Gehrig. Gehrig played in only thirteen games that year and batted .423.

On June 2, 1925, Gehrig replaced Pipp in the starting lineup. Whether Huggins intended to shake up the regulars is anybody's guess, but the shift became the stuff of baseball legend. "In the most popular version," *Sports Illustrated* recalled, "one supported in later accounts by Pipp himself (although he wasn't always consistent on the subject, either), Pipp arrived at Yankee Stadium one day in 1925 with a terrific headache. He asked the Yankee trainer for a couple of aspirin. Manager Miller Huggins noted the scene and said, 'Wally, take the day off. We'll try that kid Gehrig at first today and get you back in there tomorrow.'"

Tomorrow never came for Pipp. In a celebrated display of New York stamina, Gehrig would play the next 2,130 games—an endurance record that earned him the sobriquet "The Iron Horse" and would stand until it was shattered by Cal Ripkin, Jr., in 1995. Gehrig's streak would end only with his early-season retirement in 1939 at the age of thirty-six, after he was diagnosed with amyotrophic lateral sclerosis (ALS, also known as Lou Gehrig's disease). "I might have been given a bad break, but I've got an awful lot to live for" the self-proclaimed "luckiest man on the face of this earth" said that July 4, Lou Gehrig Appreciation Day. He died two years later.

A month after Pipp had his headache, his skull was fractured by a practice pitch, and later that season, he was traded to Cincinnati. Of his decision to sit out the June 2, 1925, game, Pipp later said: "I took the two most expensive aspirin in history."

·54·

"To City" Sign

The "Outer" Boroughs

The city seen from the Queensboro Bridge," F. Scott Fitzgerald wrote in *The Great Gatsby,* "is always the city seen for the first time, in its first wild promise of all the mystery and the beauty in the world."

Talk about forgotten boroughs! Fitzgerald was facing Manhattan at the time, with his back literally and figuratively to Queens, one of the four stepchildren of the consolidation of Greater New York in 1898. Before then, "The City" was indeed Manhattan, coterminous with New York County and New York City (and distinguished from the City of Brooklyn). No wonder the so-called outer boroughs have suffered an inferiority complex ever since.

Well after 1898, certainly for half a century or more, signs on highways, subways, and elevated train lines in Brooklyn, Queens, and the Bronx (the only borough almost entirely on the mainland) pointed tauntingly "To City," as if the outliers were merely out-of-towners. Sure, Manhattan generates most of the real estate tax revenue and city income tax and is home to Wall Street, Broadway theaters, corporate headquarters, and the most famous museums. And where else would the *Sex and the City* bus tour fete the show's fans? But

Manhattan ranks third in population (only the Bronx and Staten Island have fewer residents), although it's the most densely populated and commuters nearly double its population on weekdays, and fifth in land area. Even Central Park is only the city's fifth largest park. Manhattan doesn't even have a professional baseball or football stadium.

Yet if New York is Oz, as the columnist Pete Hamill has written, Manhattan is undeniably its Emerald City. Each borough has its own cast, often anachronistic: the Bronx, a former symbol of urban blight; Queens, the blue-collar Archie Bunker bedroom borough (now the most variegated county in the nation); Brooklyn, the home to real New York attitude—"Leaving Brooklyn: Fuhgeddaboudit," the official signs say—and the late, lamented Dodgers; and Staten Island, the bucolic borough that most closely resembles the suburbs but has, like the city's suburbs, been growing more diverse.

Manhattan was always different, even before the Lower East Side became the East Village and Hamilton Heights gained a cachet that West Harlem did not. In a century, fewer than a half dozen of New York's sixteen mayors have hailed from outside Manhattan. The disproportionate damage inflicted by snowstorms and hurricanes on the boroughs with less than sufficient mass transit worsened the real and perceived divide. The festering inferiority complex periodically boiled over into resentment against Manhattan's hypocritical "limousine liberals," who neglected the other half in this perennial tale of two cities. Symbolic of these iniquities to diehard New Yorkers who hailed from outside Manhattan were those "To City" signs.

Perhaps the most famous were two-foot-square DayGlo versions installed on Queens Boulevard in the 1960s by a contractor to detour traffic during reconstruction. The signs outlasted the repair project, a perennial thumb in the eye in a borough where nobody said they came from Queens, but typically identified with their local parish (much like Brooklynites would volunteer the name of their high school).

"In Queens we never thought of ourselves as coming from New York City," said Mario M. Cuomo, the former governor and proud son of the borough. "Manhattan was New York."

Things may be changing, as would-be or former Manhattanites gravitate to hip neighborhoods in Brownstone Brooklyn, Williamsburg, Dumbo, Carroll Gardens, and other communities pioneered by artists and gentrified with warp speed. When Bill de Blasio of Brooklyn was elected in 2013, he was the first mayor from outside Manhattan in forty years.

The city may be metamorphosing from a smug symbol of Manhattan exceptionalism to an "other borough" metaphor for elitism and pretentiousness. Overheard recently in a midtown elevator:

"Finally, I found a terrific new apartment," the first young man said.

"Congratulations!" his friend from Brooklyn replied. "That's great."

"Yeah," the lucky new homeowner replied ambivalently, "but it's on the Upper West Side."

·55·

Air Conditioner

New York Gets the Cold Shoulder

In 1902, a twenty-six-year-old junior engineer for a furnace company installed a maze of fans, ducts, and pipes in the Sackett-Wilhelms Lithographing and Publishing Co. printing plant in Williamsburg, Brooklyn. His goal: to lower the humidity that made paper expand and to speed the ink-drying process. By inventing a machine that blew air over cold coils, he succeeded beyond his wildest expectations. Willis Carrier perfected air-conditioning.

Carrier, a farmer's son from upstate New York, was said to have conceived the technique while waiting for a train and observing a fog bank rolling over the station platform. He compressed ammonia until it liquefied, then forced it to evaporate and distributed the resulting cool air by fan. Carrier's invention transformed not only New York's skyline but also America's demographics—largely at the city's expense.

Windowless offices and work spaces were now possible. Movie theaters became air-cooled oases. Department stores and other retail outlets improved summer sales. The workplace became more productive. Vast heat-generating computer facilities became practicable, fostering today's information technology revolution. But air-conditioning would also drive many New Yorkers indoors during the summer, and into their air-conditioned cars, diminishing the stoop and street-life social culture that urbanists like Jane Jacobs celebrated, and enhancing the popularity of television.

Life in what Kevin Phillips dubbed the Sunbelt in 1969 suddenly became more bearable, precipitating a population shift that amounted to an exodus, as older white New Yorkers retired to the South and Southwest, and magnets for employment—from manufacturing to white-collar back-office work—lured jobs from the Northeast. By the 1950s, sales of electric individual-room air conditioners (invented earlier but delayed by the Depression and World War II) soared.

More than a million were sold in 1953 alone—speeding the tilt to the South and West and producing an inexorable slide in New York's political clout in Congress and in the electoral college. The Sunbelt accounted for 28 percent of the nation's population in 1950. By 2000 it comprised 40 percent. As a result, New York State's congressional delegation shrank from a numerical peak of 45 of the total 435 seats in the 1940s to 27 when Congress convened in 2013.

New York's modest population growth since 2000 has paled in comparison to that of a number of states in the South and West. In New York State, virtually all the growth was driven by New York City and several suburban counties. The decline in the state's delegation affected New York's influence not only in Congress, but also in the Electoral College. Don't blame it all on air-conditioning—but unless you count transplants like Dwight D. Eisenhower and Richard M. Nixon, no New Yorker has been elected president since Franklin D. Roosevelt in 1944.

That
Something Different
in Refrigeration

FOR two years Famous Players have employed engineers to study the practical application of refrigeration to the theatre.

Research in the smaller theatres proved the simplicity of a tie-up with the ordinary ice system.

The trick was to make the air cold, but also to eliminate that clammy, damp and humid atmosphere that persists with the ordinary ice-plant.

Paramount now presents to the people of New York, at the Rivoli, the final and perfected result—the manufacturing of *ideal* weather.

69 degrees all the time. *But crisp, dry and invigorating air, too!*

The RIVOLI
NEW YORK
*Your Ideal
Summer Resort*

·56·

Ticker Tape

Final Words from a Crash

Wall Street has been synonymous with American finance—and has defined New York to the rest of the world—since May 17, 1792, when twenty-four brokers convened under a buttonwood tree and agreed to regulate the stock market. Until the exchange itself went public in 2006, members were limited to 1,366 seats, which traded for upward of $1 million each (depending on market conditions, they might be priced higher or lower than the going rate for taxi medallions).

By the end of the nineteenth century, trading volume was increasing exponentially. It tripled between 1896 and 1899 alone, then doubled by 1901. To accommodate the growth, the Stock Exchange commissioned a neoclassic headquarters designed by George B. Post, which opened at 18 Broad Street in 1903. The trading floor, half the size of a football field, measured 109 by 140 feet under a 72-foot-high ceiling. The 90-ton pediment, designed by John Quincy Adams Ward (he also sculpted the statue of George Washington across the street at Federal Hall), featured a 22-foot figure flanked by representations of Agriculture and Mining and Science, Industry and Invention, and waves symbolizing the exchange's global maritime scope. It is titled *Integrity Protecting the Works of Man.* Apparently, integrity was insufficient protection. The weighty marble figures, ravaged by pollution and flaws, were replaced in 1936 by lead-coated replicas.

A paper strip running through a stock ticker (the name reflected the sound the machine made) produced ticker tape. Introduced in New York in 1867 by Edward A. Calahan, who worked for the American Telegraph Co., it has been described as the earliest medium of digital electronic communication. It would endure for fully a century, elating and terrifying brokers glued to their tickers around the country and providing fodder for the distinctive confetti that distinguished New York's ticker-tape parades up the Canyon of Heroes in Lower Broadway. The original machines used Morse code; Thomas Edison's ticker, developed in 1869, printed out one alphanumeric character per second. (Nowadays, trading algorithms depend on information flashed in milliseconds.)

Arguably, Wall Street's worst moment was Tuesday, October 29, 1929. Shouts of "sell" drowned out the opening bell. In the first half hour alone, three million shares were traded; $2 million in value evaporated. When the market closed at 3:00 P.M. that day, it had lost $14 billion (over $300 billion in today's dollars). A record 16.4 million shares had been traded, recorded on fifteen thousand miles of ticker tape that registered a net loss in the Dow Jones Industrial Average of 12 percent. The last ribbon of ticker tape, which could accommodate 285 words a minute, ran hours late. The final two words, appropriately enough, were "Good Night." The market would not recover to its pre-crash level until 1954.

TOTAL SALES TODAY ... GOOD NIGHT OCT
16,388,700. 29 1929.

Chrysler Building Spire

Race to the Roof

Detroit is still synonymous with the automobile industry, but New York played a starring role, too: Broadway was dotted with showrooms (they have since moved west to Eleventh Avenue) and, as an automotive headquarters city, punctuated by trophy skyscrapers: the General Motors Building (the old one at Broadway and Fifty-Seventh and the newer one on Fifth Avenue and Fifty-Ninth Street), the Fisk Tire Building, the New York General Building (the General Tire name required the editing of only two letters on the old New York Central headquarters on Park Avenue), and of course, the Chrysler Building.

"I like to build things. I like to do things," Walter P. Chrysler would say, reasoning that "every new development, new highway, railroad, steamship line, building operation, whether it be a drainage project in old Greece or a new water system in Peru, means an added use of the automobile." To showcase his company, he took over construction of the art deco Chrysler Building in 1930 from the developer of Coney Island's Dreamland, but he paid for the building personally so his children would inherit it. Designed by William Van Alen, the brick tower features gargoyles on the thirty-first floor, modeled on Chrysler radiator caps, and eagles on the sixty-first. The stainless-steel crown consists of seven radiating terraced sunburst arches. The seventy-first floor contains its highest occupied office space.

Ground was broken on September 19, 1928, during a race to build the world's tallest skyscraper. H. Craig Severance's 40 Wall Street was the apparent winner—until Van Alen surreptitiously spirited a 125-foot spire inside the Chrysler Building's steel frame. When it was completed on May 20, 1930, the spire elevated the Chrysler Building to 1,048 feet, making it the world's tallest building and the first man-made structure to surpass a thousand feet. But only eleven months later, it was exceeded by the Empire State Building.

The land on which it was built is owned by Cooper Union for the Advancement of Science and Art. The footprint is a trapezoid, because the eastern boundary predates John Randel, Jr.'s street grid, adopted as the Commissioner's Plan of 1811. The Abu Dhabi Investment Council is now the majority owner of the building.

Walter Chrysler died at his Kings Point, Long Island, waterfront estate in 1940 (it later became part of the U.S. Merchant Marine Academy). He is buried in an ornate mausoleum in Sleepy Hollow Cemetery in Westchester.

For bragging rights among New York skyscrapers today, the Chrysler Building is tied for fourth with the New York Times Building. The new World Trade Center is first, followed by the Empire State and the Bank of America Tower on West Forty-Second Street. The Chrysler retains one architectural distinction: it remains the world's tallest brick building (an estimated 3,826,000 bricks form the non-loadbearing walls). Even if it is no longer the tallest and is typically overshadowed by the Empire State, it remains one of the city's most beloved icons.

·58·

Artichoke

The Fruits of Organized Crime

*C*ynara scolymus, aka the artichoke, is native to the Mediterranean. So was Ciro Terranova. Long before ordinary New Yorkers had ever heard of the Black Hand or the Mafia, Terranova had imported the latest incarnation of ethnic crime from Corleone in Sicily. Terranova—the name itself suggesting a hearty transplant—also imported artichokes, an original staple in minestrone soup, from California. Headquartered in East Harlem, then an Italian enclave, he cornered the market, terrorized merchants into carrying his produce, and earned the sobriquet "The Artichoke King."

In New York and other big cities, homegrown organized crime typically was accompanied by an ethnic dimension—beginning with nativist gangs and later encompassing virtually every immigrant group, each of which imposed its own distinctive cast. Irish and Jewish gangs proliferated in their respective ghettos, supplanted—as the sons and grandsons of gangsters graduated into medicine and law and Wall Street and moved to the suburbs—by blacks, Puerto Ricans, Asians, Colombians, and Russians.

Virtually no group was exempt from the curse of criminality, but none captured the public's imagination more than the Italians (they had the best nick-

names). It would take Fiorello La Guardia, an Italian-American (and part Jewish) mayor—so sensitive about stereotypes that he banned organ grinders and their monkeys from the city—to challenge their stranglehold over immigrant neighborhoods and entire industries.

Terranova was larger than life, almost literally. He was the sole survivor of a trio of racketeer siblings (the other two had been gunned down) and the stepbrother of Giuseppe "Clutch Hand" Morello. He was the father of ten children; moved them into a million-dollar home (in today's dollars) on Peace Street in Pelham, just across the Westchester border; and drove an armored limousine. He also figured in the unsolved robbery of a testimonial dinner he was attending on behalf of a Bronx magistrate. The dinner triggered sweeping investigations into the judiciary by Samuel Seabury, a descendant of the first Episcopal bishop in America. Seabury's crusading commission forced the resignation of Mayor James J. Walker and laid the political groundwork for the election of La Guardia.

Introduced by the blare of uniformed police buglers, La Guardia went to the heart of the matter in 1935. He banned the sale, display, and possession of artichokes in New York City in an attempt to topple Terranova's empire. "There is only one way of breaking a racket," he declared, "and that is either to remove the source or remove the individuals from the scene of operations. In the retail markets we removed the individuals. In the wholesale traffic of the commodity we are going to remove the source."

Terranova might also have been the only person threatened with arrest if he ventured into the city. La Guardia exiled him to Westchester. The threat was fulfilled when he was charged with vagrancy in 1937. He died at age forty-nine, supposedly penniless, after a stroke.

·59·

Tree of Hope

Making Their Own Luck

Never mess with show business superstitions. At the tail end of the Harlem Renaissance in 1934, Ralph Cooper, Sr., launched the Wednesday weekly Amateur Night at the Apollo Theater on West 125th Street. Those performances would become the springboard for generations of musical stars, including Ella Fitzgerald (she was fifteen when she became one of the first Amateur Night winners), James Brown, Diana Ross, and Stevie Wonder, and a precursor for modern incarnations like *American Idol.*

Amateur Night was broadcast live over WMCA radio and carried on a national network. The performers had free rein, and the rules for the audience were simple, Cooper once recalled. "'If you like the performer, cheer,'" he said. "'You know how to cheer, don't you?' And the audience let out a roar that rattled windows all over Harlem." Currently, auditions are open to performers over the age of five and "should be in good taste" and without profanity. Performers have up to ninety seconds to demonstrate their bona fides, and judges will review the first three hundred acts "if time permits."

Seventh Avenue was known locally as the Boulevard of Dreams. The Harlem Renaissance thrived there for about two decades, beginning roughly in 1918. It overlapped the Great Migration of African-Americans from the South (blacks accounted for about 100,000 of New York's 4.7 million residents in 1910 and more than 450,000 of 7 million New Yorkers by 1940, increasing their share of the population from under 2 percent to over 6 percent). The Apollo opened in 1913 as a segregated venue. Harlem's most exclusive clubs featured black performers and mostly white audiences. Those forces merged in an explosion of culture that helped forge a new black identity and set the stage for the civil rights movement in the 1950s and beyond. The Renaissance, also known as the "New Negro Movement," marked what James Weldon Johnson described as the "flowering of Negro literature." Figures associated with the Renaissance included Countee Cullen, W. E. B. Du Bois, Marcus Garvey, Zora Neale Hurston, Langston Hughes, Alain Locke, and Claude McKay.

Good luck, legend had it, would come to performers who paused under the branches of an elm tree that stood on Seventh Avenue between 131st and 132nd Streets, flanked by the Lafayette Theater (where Cooper's original Harlem Amateur Hour debuted in 1933) and Connie's Inn. When the tree was removed so the avenue could be widened, Cooper brought an eighteen-inch-diameter slice of the trunk, about a foot high and he had it mounted on a pedestal at stage right just in front of the curtain, so it is visible to audiences. Contestants still touch it for good luck before they perform.

·60·

King Kong

A Beauty and the Beasts

Let's face it," Godzilla says to King Kong in a *New Yorker* cartoon while they nonchalantly stroll past scenes of havoc as terrified Manhattanites flee before them. "The city's in our blood."

Like so many other New Yorkers, the scaly monster and his furry friend were drawn from someplace else. Manhattan has been a magnet for mayhem and creative destruction. On seeing the skyline for the first time, H. G. Wells was said to have proclaimed: "What a ruin it will make!" In the original *The Day the Earth Stood Still,* an awestruck cabbie says, "My ol' lady was right. We shoulda got a place in the country."

Upheaval of one sort or another was taken for granted—even celebrated—by everyone from W. E. B. Du Bois to Upton Sinclair, from Henry James (who pronounced it "a provisional city") to Orson Welles and Joan Didion (she called it "the shining and perishable dream itself").

"We destroy New York on film and paper by telling stories of clear and present dangers, with causes and effects, villains and heroes, to make our world more comprehensible than it has become," said Max Page, a University of Massachusetts professor, who wrote *The City's End.*

New York was too big for King Kong, at least for the eighteen-inch version (scaled at one inch to the foot) who presided from his aerie on Skull Island in the Pacific in the film of the same name. Dense Manhattan, like an overgrown jungle, demanded a twenty-four-inch-tall metal armature sheathed in latex and rabbit fur. The spurt in skyscrapers shifted the venue of his final ascent in 1933 from the New York Life Building to the Chrysler Building and, ultimately, to the Empire State Building (and in a later film to the World Trade Center; a forthcoming stage version features a twenty-foot-tall ape).

"Here is the skyline at its most elemental, as a kind of primeval mountain range," James Sanders, an architect, wrote of King Kong's Manhattan vista in *Celluloid Skyline*. And, Sanders added, "how better to convey the end of the world than to show the destruction of its best known place."

Before going on his rampage, which includes prematurely razing the Sixth Avenue El, King Kong stars onstage in a Broadway theater. When a woman wonders what the audience is going to witness, her companion replies, "I hear it's kind of a giant gorilla." Just then, a man rushing to his seat rudely tramples her toe. To which the woman exclaims, "Gee, ain't we got enough of them in New York?"

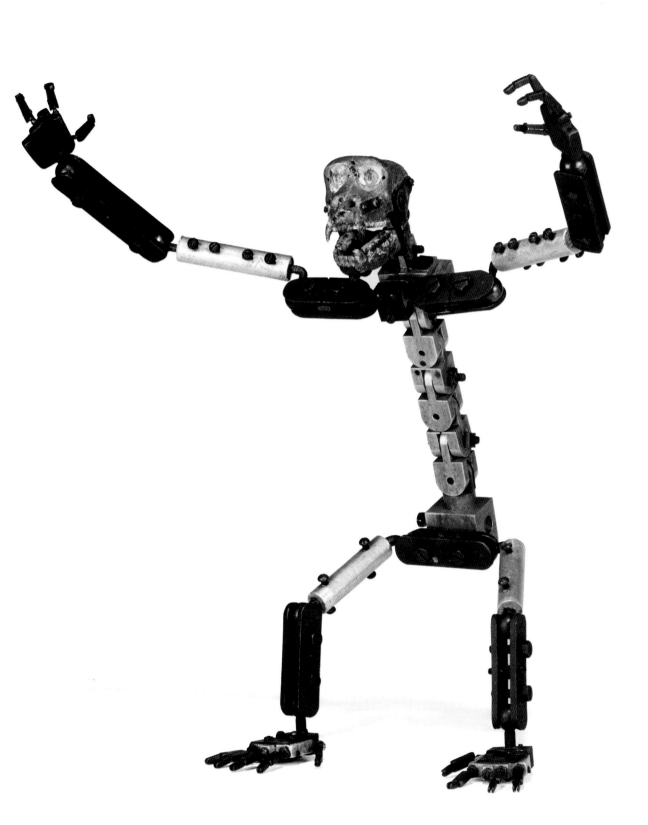

·61·

First Houses

Gimme Shelter

It took a Republican mayor to embrace a Socialist initiative and enlist a blue-blooded Democratic president with a New Deal bankroll to his cause. Clearing slums for parks was one thing. Embracing the European model and transforming vacant tracts and blighted tenements into publicly subsidized housing was quite another.

Fiorello H. La Guardia did just that, spurred by the Public Housing Conference founded in 1932 and its goal of creating a city Housing Authority to clear slums and build housing that working families could afford. "This is boondoggling Exhibit A," he declared unabashedly at the formal dedication of First Houses in 1935, "and we're proud of it."

First Houses was the first public, low-income housing project in the nation. It was hailed by Governor Herbert H. Lehman as "socially imperative and economically sound" and, in the depths of the Depression, relied on a labor force comprised mostly of men on relief. In praising the federal government for its first foray into housing, La Guardia also saluted the members of his own Housing Authority: "Where can you find a housing board to equal it: an idealist on housing, a social worker, a Catholic priest and a Socialist."

The result was four- and five-story, mostly three-room walk-ups that had been intended as gut renovations of existing tenements but wound up being built from scratch. The eight brick buildings, which flank an inner courtyard, are bordered by First Avenue and Avenue A, in the heart of the congested Lower East Side. Every room in the 122-apartment complex, which took only nine months to build, had an outside window (while construction costs exceeded expectations, the rent came in at $6.05 a room, about two-thirds of what comparable apartments cost; income

limits were set at five times the rent). The average income of the first 120 families chosen as tenants from more than 3,800 applications was $23.20 a week.

"Private capital has never in its life spent a dime to build a house for a poor person," said Harry L. Hopkins, the Works Progress Administrator, as his regional representative presented a ceremonial key to First Houses to the Housing Authority Chairman, Langdon Post. The apartments, Post said, were "the first dwellings predicated upon the philosophy that sunshine, space and air are minimum housing requirements to which every American is entitled, no matter how small his income."

Today the New York City Housing Authority manages an inventory of nearly 180,000 apartments in 334 developments. More than 600,000 New Yorkers live in Housing Authority apartments or private apartments subsidized with federal vouchers administered by the Authority. More than 200,000 individuals and families are awaiting placement in the coveted 5,000 to 6,000 Housing Authority apartments that become vacant annually. Turnover is slow. Until 1999, First Houses still included one of the project's original tenants.

·62·

Time Capsule

The Fair to End All Fairs

A just machine to make big decisions
Programmed by fellows with compassion and vision
We'll be clean when their work is done
We'll be eternally free yes and eternally young
What a beautiful world this'll be
What a glorious time to be free.

Tomorrow came early to New York in 1939. The New York World's Fair opened on April 30 that year, marking the 150th anniversary of George Washington's inauguration in New York and heralding "The World of Tomorrow" with the delusional lyrics of a Gershwin theme song, "Dawn of a New Day." Four months later, dawn broke in Europe with a bang: Nazi tanks and troops roared into Poland, and the world was once again at war.

Over two years, an estimated forty-four million visitors—equal to a third of the nation's population—visited the international and commercial pavilions in Flushing Meadows, Queens, a former swampy ash heap immortalized in *The Great*

Gatsby and transformed first into the fairgrounds and then into a permanent greensward by parks impresario Robert Moses.

While it was timed to the past, the World's Fair was also motivated by a more immediate goal: to lift the city and the nation out of the lingering doldrums of the Great Depression. Its thrust was the celebration of future promise. A nearly seven-foot, six-inch copper "time capsule" (the term was coined by G. Edward Pendray, a Westinghouse Electric Corp. publicist, who also minted the term "Laundromat") was stuffed with ephemera that would enlighten distant generations about New York's grit and determination to seize the new dawn, whenever it arrived.

The capsule contained seeds, an RKO newsreel, a can opener, a fountain pen, golf balls, a Mickey Mouse watch, a pack of cigarettes, coins, a diagram that showed where each of the thirty-three sounds of English originate in the oral cavity, and a microfilmed "Book of Record" describing "all the principal categories of our thought, activity and accomplishment." Included were the *Encyclopaedia*

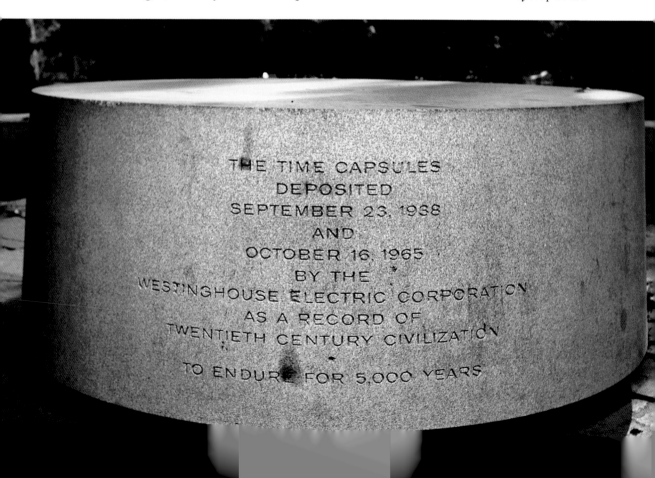

Britannica, True Confessions magazine, lyrics to "Flat Foot Floogie," and fairly gloomy messages specially written by the novelist and social critic Thomas Mann, the physicist Robert Andrews Millikan, and Albert Einstein.

"Any one who thinks about the future must live in fear and terror," Einstein wrote. "This is due to the fact that the intelligence and character of the masses are incomparably lower than the intelligence and character of the few who produce something valuable for the community. I trust that posterity will read these statements with a feeling of proud and justified superiority."

Mann lamented, "We know now that the idea of the future as a 'better world' was a fallacy of the doctrine of progress."

Millikan, citing the simmering conflicts between representative government and despotism, was more equivocal: "If the rational, scientific, progressive principles win out in this struggle there is a possibility of a warless, golden age ahead for mankind," he wrote. "If the reactionary principles of despotism triumph now and in the future, the future history of mankind will repeat the sad story of war and oppression as in the past."

Their messages contrasted vividly with the opening of the theme song:

> *Sound the brass, roll the drum,*
> *To the world of tomorrow we come.*
> *See the sun through the grey—*
> *It's the dawn of a new day!*

The torpedo-shaped capsule was buried fifty feet below the park on September 23, 1938. One sign of the fair organizers' implacable faith in the future: it is scheduled to be opened in 6939. A warning inscribed on the capsule urges anyone who unearths it prematurely to "not wantonly disturb it, for to do so would be to deprive the people of that era of the legacy here left them. Cherish it therefore in a safe place."

·63·

Cyclotron

Building a Bomb

"Tell me dear," the letter to New Mexico postmarked from the Lower East Side began, "does the 'Manhattan' in your address mean that all the men there are from this district originally, or that they're scheduled to come here, or is it just there for the lack of a better address. Do you know yet what you'll be doing? Dear why all the secrecy this time?"

It wasn't called the Manhattan Project for nothing. The origin of the name was less secretive than serendipitous. The Manhattan District of the Army Corps of Engineers opened its first office in Manhattan because the city was home to a critical mass of scientists and matériel, as well as the communications network to organize the biggest government project ever conceived: the design, construction, and detonation of an atomic bomb. With the Nazis overrunning Europe and the Soviet Union poised to become a cold war rival, the need for secrecy was manifest—a reality that would become all too obvious shortly to the letter-writer, the wife of atomic spy David Greenglass, who was an army machinist at Los Alamos, New Mexico, where the prototype of the bomb was being developed.

In 1942, Colonel James C. Marshall of the Army Corps of Engineers opened his temporary headquarters on the eighteenth floor of 270 Broadway, across from

City Hall, close to the base of the corps' North Atlantic Division, to Stone & Webster, the principal contractor, and to scientists at Columbia University, where a pioneering cyclotron was splitting atoms in the basement of Pupin Hall.

As a cradle of atomic research, New York would play a large part in ending the war. The city was instrumental in waging war, too (from M1 carbines assembled by IBM to penicillin manufactured in Brooklyn by Charles Pfizer & Co., from the Office of Strategic Services, the CIA's predecessor, in Rockefeller Center, to the submarine net built by John A. Roebling's Sons Co. and strung from Staten Island). "New York wasn't generally on the front lines—though German U-boats sank tankers in local waters," Edward Rothstein wrote in *The New York Times,* "but with its port, manufacturing ship building and strategic military centers it made the front lines possible" once Pearl Harbor all but obliterated isolationism.

In 1939, Columbia's thirty-ton, seven-foot-tall cyclotron's electromagnets sent particles spinning at 25,000 miles per second in spiral paths before smashing them into targets. A year later, the cyclotron was used to identify fissionable uranium, which suggested the possibility of a chain reaction. (As it happened, 2,006 steel drums containing 1,250 tons of high-grade uranium ore—some of which ended up in the bomb—had been far-sightedly gathered in a Port Richmond, Staten Island, vegetable oil warehouse by Edgar Sengier, a managing director of Union Miniére, a Belgian company with offices in the Cunard Building at 25 Broadway.) The Columbia cyclotron was retired in 1965. Several plaques in Pupin Hall celebrate its history without referring even once to the atomic bomb.

·64·

"This Land"

The Forgotten Borough

No man is an island, John Donne memorably wrote, but what about nearly *five hundred thousand* men, women, and children? What about their fifty-eight-square-mile outcropping in New York Harbor, its population bigger than Miami's or Sacramento's or Atlanta's? It has been lamented as "The Forgotten Borough" of New York City (the third largest in land area after Queens and Brooklyn) and has been demeaned for its utter isolation (it is the only borough self-contained on a single island; three bridges connect it to New Jersey, one to Brooklyn).

Staten Island was named by Dutch settlers in the seventeenth century to honor their patron, the States General, or Dutch parliament. If Staten Islanders still claim to be doomed to orphanhood, the island's political provenance was often disputed, too. Just a few hundred yards across the Arthur Kill creek from New Jersey, it is a mile from the closest New York landfall, the Brooklyn shoreline. Legend has it that New York nearly lost Staten Island to New Jersey in the seventeenth century, until a British captain circumnavigated it in a single day (what would second prize have been?). It remains known as Richmond County (for the illegitimate son of King Charles II) and was fully incorporated into Greater New York following a referendum in which the largest margin of victory was among hopeful Staten Islanders.

178

God Blessed America

This Land Was made For You & me

This land is your land, this land is my land
From California to the New York Island,
From the Redwood Forest, to the Gulf stream waters,
    God blessed America for me.

As I went walking that ribbon of highway
And saw above me that endless skyway,
And saw below me the golden valley, I said:
    God blessed America for me.

I roamed and rambled, and followed my footsteps
To the sparkling sands of her diamond deserts,
And all around me, a voice was sounding:
    God blessed America for me.

Was a big high wall there that tried to stop me
A sign was painted said: Private Property.
But on the back side it didn't say nothing —
    God blessed America for me.

When the sun come shining, then I was strolling
In wheat fields waving, and dust clouds rolling;
The voice was chanting as the fog was lifting:
    God blessed America for me.

One bright sunny morning in the shadow of the steeple
By the Relief office I saw my people —
As they stood hungry, I stood there wondering if
    God blessed America for me.

          * all you can write is
            what you see.

                    Woody G.
                    N.Y., N.Y., N.Y.
                    Feb. 23, 1940
                    43rd st & 6th Ave.,
                    Hanover House

original copy
of this song

© Woody Guthrie Publications, Inc.

But the marriage was rocky from the beginning. The influx of off-islanders, following construction of the Verrazano-Narrows Bridge from Brooklyn in 1964 (still the longest span in the Western Hemisphere), only made matters worse. White refugees from the other boroughs, driven by the real and perceived downsides of urban congestion and diversity, discovered on Staten Island the deficiencies of suburban isolation and homogeneity. The borough's political clout was eviscerated in 1986 with the abolition of the city's Board of Estimate, which had granted the Staten Island borough president the same number of votes as his four other borough colleagues. (The borough is now represented by only three of the fifty-one members of the City Council.)

In 1993 a secession referendum drew enough votes from Staten Islanders to oust David N. Dinkins, the city's first black mayor, and supplant him with a Republican former prosecutor, Rudolph W. Giuliani, who redeemed their trust by restoring free service on the Staten Island Ferry and shuttering the reviled Fresh Kills Landfill (10,000 tons of garbage daily grew to be 140 feet high, making it the highest spot on the Atlantic coastline).

Even as growth slowed, the population—less poor and more white than the rest of the city and still one third of Italian ancestry—became more diverse (Jews from the Soviet Union settled there, and Liberian refugees established an enclave). It is the only borough with its own enduring daily newspaper and without a city-owned primary care hospital. Hurricane Sandy, striking with disproportionate impact, left Staten Islanders even more isolated.

Things had gone from bad to verse. In 1944, when Woody Guthrie revised his original lyrics to "This Land," he struck the borough's name from his song. Worse, he substituted the ambiguous "New York Island" (the "I" remained capitalized), which no doubt meant Manhattan, where the original lyrics were handwritten on February 23, 1940, by Guthrie while he was living at the Hanover House hotel just off Times Square.

·65·

La Guardia Reading Comics

The Greatest Mayor

New Yorkers generally measure their mayors by three criteria: the challenges they inherited, the resources they mustered to meet those challenges, and the legacy of their accomplishments and failures. By those measures, coupled with his sheer force of personality, Fiorello H. La Guardia, the city's ninety-ninth mayor, is widely considered New York's greatest.

In 1934 he inherited a Depression and a city demoralized by political corruption. A street-smart Republican, he forged a mutually beneficial alliance with a patrician Democratic president, Franklin D. Roosevelt, to overhaul and revive the city by transforming it into a showcase of New Deal urban development that transcended petty local politics, vested interests, and individual agendas.

"New York in depression and war was a city of decidedly *public* ambitions," wrote Mason B. Williams, a historian: a city of libraries, parks, local health clinics, free adult education, model housing, and "bridges and tunnels and airports intended to integrate the five boroughs and to link the city to the metropolitan region and the wider world." The bond between La Guardia and Roosevelt (abetted by the mayor's construction coordinator, Robert Moses) got those public works built as in no other place. No coincidence that New Yorkers can take the Franklin D. Roosevelt Drive en route to La Guardia Airport.

In addition to that palpable legacy, La Guardia demonstrated that the city was governable again (just as two of his successors, Edward I. Koch and Rudolph W. Giuliani, would do decades later, overcoming similar crises of confidence).

One of La Guardia's greatest assets—and an occasional liability—was his outsize personality. He was called "The Little Flower," a play on his first name and his height (he stood barely five-two), but he was no shrinking violet.

When La Guardia took office for his first four-year term as mayor on January 1, 1934, he had risen higher on the political ladder than any other American of Italian descent. Despite his histrionics—maybe because of them—he was much beloved by most constituents, who reelected him as mayor twice.

Nothing endeared him to New Yorkers more enduringly than his performance during a seventeen-day newspaper delivery drivers' strike in 1945. Interrupting his regular Sunday radio broadcast that July 1, he invited adult listeners to gather their children around the radio and then began reading the latest *Dick Tracy* comic strip from the *Sunday News*. He summarized the plot to that point, imitated voices of the various characters, and at the end left his audience with a moral: "Say, children, what does it all mean?" he asked rhetorically. "It means that dirty money never brings any luck! No, dirty money always brings sorrow and sadness and misery and disgrace." Reading the comics with his trademark gusto distinguished La Guardia from stuffy politicians then and now. He was a real-life hero.

·66·

Levittown House

Manufactured Dreams

Brooklyn Heights is regarded as America's first nineteenth-century suburb (Jacques Cortelyou, a surveyor, commuted from a bluff overlooking the Narrows to Bowling Green as early as 1656), but Levittown has been synonymous with suburbia beginning in the mid-twentieth century. William J. Levitt's paradigmatic, mass-produced developments fostered an exodus of white homeowner wannabes from New York in the postwar years, many of them veterans returning to start families and seeking to fulfill the American dream of an affordable home with a meticulously mowed front lawn and a backyard.

The racial calculus was not coincidental. Levittown would not sell to blacks. "As a Jew, I have no room in my heart for racial prejudice," Levitt explained. "But the plain fact is that most whites prefer not to live in mixed communities. This attitude may be wrong morally, and someday it may change. I hope it will." In 1950 New York City was home to 7.1 million whites, by 1980 to only 3.7 million. Many left for places like Levittown.

Levittown was not only white; it was green. With no stoops or front porches and with houses occupying just 12 percent of the lot, the lawn was, according to Abraham Levitt (the patriarch, whose company built seventeen thousand cookie-

cutter homes in four years, beginning in 1947), a cue to visitors as to what type of people lived there. "A fine carpet of green grass," he wrote in his weekly local gardening column, "stamps the inhabitants as good neighbors, as desirable citizens." A covenant in the deeds required lawns to be manicured once a week between April and November.

Fortunately, postwar prefabricated housing coincided with another innovation vital to suburbanization. After all, would any red-blooded New Yorker in his right mind ever have moved to the suburbs without the power lawn mower? (Coincidentally, the "Cradle of the American Lawn Mower" happened to be just up the Hudson in Newburgh.) According to American-lawns.com, after driving tanks and jeeps and bombers, fighting men were in no mood to cut the grass with a nineteenth-century lawn mower. That was women's work: "Women in mass stood up and in a quiet revolt pointed their respective husbands towards hardware stores across American in search of the power mower. Things haven't been the same since."

Only a month after construction was announced and before the first concrete slab foundations were even finished, Levitt & Sons announced that all two thousand of the four-room 750-square-foot homes it was assembling in a former potato field in Hempstead, Long Island, had been spoken for. By July 1948, the company was mass-producing thirty houses a day to meet the unprecedented demand.

Rent was originally $60 a month, with an option to buy at $6,990. Most of the homes have since been expanded, but one of the few original ones, 52 Oak Tree Lane, was designated a town landmark in the 1990s.

By 2010 whites still comprised more than 80 percent of the nearly 52,000 residents. Blacks made up less than 1 percent. In New York City, meanwhile, the ratio had shifted dramatically. The share of non-Hispanic whites had shrunk to 33 percent. The share of blacks more than doubled, to about 25 percent.

·67·

Cotton Picker

Deus ex Machina

During the Great Migration between 1910 and 1940, about 1.5 million African-Americans left the South. In the following three decades, the second great migration to New York and other Northern cities drew three times that many.

Much of the second migration coincided with the proliferation of a labor-saving device that both spurred the exodus and was viewed, in part, as a response to it: the mechanical cotton picker. The device emancipated black workers from backbreaking labor and its inevitable by-products: insufficient education, suppressed standards of living, and, as one historian wrote, the miserable "tedium of unchanging expectations" about a sharecropping system that dated to the Civil War.

Some Southerners feared the impact of the machine on those who were already prone to unemployment. In 1936 the *Jackson (MS) Daily News,* pronouncing the picker all too practical, warned: "Imagine, if you can, 500,000 Negroes in Mississippi just now lolling around on cabin galleries or loafing on the streets." But a decade later, blacks had been lured north by factory jobs during World War II, and those who were left behind and feared displacement by the mechanical cotton picker did not loll around; they headed north, too. In 1940 New York was home to fewer than five hundred thousand African-Americans. By 1960, the black population had more than doubled as a share of the total and in sheer numbers—the biggest two-decade numerical increase before or since (after 2000, the number of black New Yorkers began to decline, for the first time since the draft riots during the Civil War, as more moved to the suburbs and to the South). The black population peaked at nearly 29 percent in 1990 (a year after the city elected its first black mayor, David N. Dinkins). By 2000, Hispanic New Yorkers outnumbered blacks.

Patents for cotton harvesters dated to the mid-nineteenth-century, but the man generally credited with the invention was John Daniel Rust, a onetime cotton picker who, in Donald Holley's definitive study, was described as the dreamer worried about the social consequences of his invention while his brother Mack, who had a degree in engineering, was more concerned with the mechanics. "I remember how cotton used to stick to my fingers when I was a boy picking in the early morning dew," John once recalled. "I jumped out of bed, found some absorbent cotton and a nail for testing. I licked the nail and twirled it in the cotton and found that it could work."

Commercial production of the mechanical cotton picker began in the late 1940s, which hastened the end of sharecropping and the need for cheap and docile labor. "The mechanization of cotton," Holley wrote, "was an essential condition for the civil rights movement in the 1950s." As much as it reshaped the South, it also vividly redefined the face of Northern cities like New York.

Robinson's Glove

"The Residue of Design"

The armed forces were still legally segregated. So were public schools. Black people could clean houses in places like Levittown but couldn't buy homes there. That was America in 1947, when a Brooklyn-based, teetotaling, Methodist Bible-quoting Republican from Ohio integrated major league baseball.

"Luck," Branch Rickey liked to say, "is the residue of design." Rickey's designs on major league baseball were nothing short of revolutionary. Before *Brown* vs. *Board of Education* outlawed school segregation, before President Harry Truman integrated the military, the Brooklyn Dodgers' president and general manager defied everyone but his truest fans by bulldozing the color barrier in major league baseball. His vessel was a stubbornly persuasive infielder named Jack Roosevelt Robinson.

Jackie Robinson was a four-letter athlete at the University of California, Los Angeles. As an army draftee, he had refused to sit in the back of a segregated bus. On August 28, 1945, Rickey signed Robinson to a minor league contract (with the Montreal Royals) for the following season and in 1947 installed him at first base for the Brooklyn Dodgers. He made the decision on merit, once recalling that a baseball box score "doesn't tell how big you are, what church you attend, what color you are, or how your father voted in the last election. It just tells what kind of baseball player you were on that particular day."

What kind of player was Robinson? "It kills me to lose," he often said. "If I'm a troublemaker, and I don't think that my temper makes me one, then it's because

I can't stand losing. That's the way I am about winning, all I ever wanted to do was finish first."

Organized baseball led by Commissioner Kennesaw Mountain Landis was against integration (no black had played in the majors since 1889). Landis died in 1944, but even before that, Rickey had persuaded the Dodgers to let him recruit "the right man" for this breakthrough role. He said he needed more than a very good player. He needed a virtuous man with the self-discipline to turn the other cheek to the predictable taunts: "I must be sure that the man was good on the field, but more dangerous to me, at that time and even now, was the wrong man off the field."

It was the right move morally, and Rickey was a deeply moral man. (As a player for the St. Louis Browns, Rickey had an unremarkable record except for allowing more stolen bases, thirteen, than any catcher in one game. As a manager, he was famous for dispensing raises more sparingly than sage advice. But when a black player for Ohio Wesleyan University was denied entry to an all-white hotel, Rickey proclaimed: "I may not be able to do something about racism in every field, but I can sure do something about it in baseball.") His decision also was commonsensical, given the changing demographics of the Brooklyn fan base and evolving views toward race after World War II—as well as the chance to recruit the best players from the Negro Leagues.

Robinson finished his first season as Rookie of the Year, with 12 homers, a league-leading 29 steals, and a .297 batting average. The Dodgers even made it to the World Series—for only the fourth time (losing, naturally, to the Yankees, though in seven games)—but integrating the Fall Classic for the first time.

Robinson, number 42, was inducted into the Baseball Hall of Fame in 1962. "The way I figured it, I was even with baseball and baseball with me," he once said. "The game had done much for me, and I had done much for it."

·69·

Jell-O Box

A Raspberry for Russia

$\mathbf{A}$ food product congealed with gelatin was patented in 1845 by Peter Cooper, the industrialist who owned a glue factory in Kips Bay, founded the Cooper Union for the Advancement of Science, and was instrumental in laying the Atlantic Cable. His patent was sold to a cough-syrup maker who, in 1897, invented a packaged version that his wife dubbed Jell-O.

A half century later, a cut-up box of Jell-O, imitation red raspberry–flavored, would figure prominently in the 1951 spy trial of the century; the case against a Manhattan couple, Julius and Ethel Rosenberg. Lower East Side parents of two young sons and Communists, the Rosenbergs were indicted vaguely for conspiracy to commit espionage, but the prosecution—and the judge—specifically accused them of stealing *the* secret to the atomic bomb and delivering it to the Soviets.

How would Ethel's brother, David Greenglass, an army machinist assigned to the secret government laboratory at Los Alamos, New Mexico, recognize the Russians' courier? "Julius took the side of a Jell-O box and cut it in an odd fashion," David's wife, Ruth, later testified. He gave her one half of the side panel and, she recalled with biblical cadence, he said the other "will be brought to you by another party and he will bear the greetings from me and you will know that I have sent him." David said, "Oh, that is very clever," to which Julius replied: "The simplest things are the cleverest."

The prop Jell-O box—the original was presumably discarded somewhere in New Mexico—introduced by an assistant prosecutor, Roy Cohn, became emblematic of the Rosenberg case (and survives in the National Archives). The trial riv-

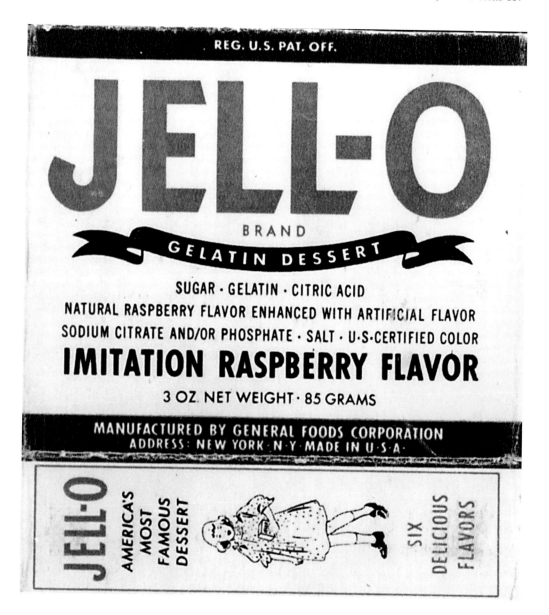

eted the nation. Considerably more testimony in the book-length trial transcript was presented about Jell-O and its packaging than about building an atomic bomb.

The Rosenbergs were convicted and executed in 1953 in a case that continues to divide the American left. It is generally accepted that Julius was guilty of the espionage conspiracy charge and that Ethel was prosecuted largely as leverage against her husband's refusal to confess or to name names. They proved more valuable to the Soviets as martyred suicide spies than as espionage agents.

The case against them—which offered proof of a Communist conspiracy but only insinuations of its scope and impact—laid the groundwork for McCarthyism and the profound and enduring damage it inflicted on New Yorkers and their institutions, in fields ranging from public education to Broadway.

The Atomic Age, as it was sometimes called, produced a social side show. School students were issued dog tags so their bodies could be identified. Civil Defense drills were regularly conducted. Yellow-and-black signs directing people to makeshift shelters from radioactive fallout proliferated (many survive). Still, it was hard to grasp the magazine illustrations of Manhattan, ground zero in any nuclear scenario, after being pulverized by a single A-bomb blast. It was easier to face that unfathomable threat in the form of something more prosaic—like, say, a Jell-O box.

·70·

Spaldeen

Having a Ball

It's bubblegum pink, a hollow, spongy two-and-a-half-inch-diameter sphere that now costs about twelve times what it did when it was introduced. It can bounce five hundred times on a concrete sidewalk or macadam pavement at fifty mph without losing its spunk. Let's forget for a moment that the manufacturer was established in 1876 by a former Boston Red Stockings pitcher, A. G. Spalding. The high-bounce ball was first made in Massachusetts, but by virtue of its ubiquity in stickball and other urban street games, the Spaldeen says New York.

The Spalding company traces the brand to 1949, when defective rubber tennis balls were removed from the assembly line before the fuzz was applied and sold to five-and-dime stores stamped with the distinctive logo: "Spalding High-Bounce Ball." They became staples of stickball (brooms for bats, manholes, and fire hydrants for bases—oh, to be a two-sewer hitter), stoopball, hit the penny, box ball, punch ball, and other imaginative games that transformed big-city streets and sidewalks into playgrounds.

The nickname, a New York pronunciation of "Spalding," was made official when the company trademarked it and the balls began to be mass-produced instead of being culled from rejected tennis balls. (The Pennsy Pinky, made by the

Penn tennis ball company, was another brand, and the merits of each are still debated. Generally, the arguments can be summed up this way: The Pinky didn't have seams; the Spaldeen was more perfectly round and bounced higher.) Production ended in 1979, when tennis ball manufacturing was shifted to Taiwan, but a steady drumbeat from nostalgic fans persuaded Spalding, now owned by Russell Brands, to market them again (starting at $1.99, compared to the original 15 cents) and now in varieties resembling a baseball and basketball.

"New York without punch ball, stickball and Spaldeens," a reader from British Columbia wrote, "is like Jersey without boredom. C'mon." Streetplay.com, a website that chronicles big-city life, called the Spaldeen "the Rosetta Stone of urban childhood fun." It joyously bounced its way into urban culture. In *The Fortress of Solitude,* Jonathan Lethem invokes the Spaldeen, recounting Dylan Ebdus's stoopball games on Dean Street in the Gowanus section of 1970s Brooklyn (Sandy Koufax played stoopball before becoming a major league pitcher, and Marv Albert, the Brooklyn-born sports announcer, built a stoop to nowhere at his suburban home because he missed the game.) In the television series *Weeds,* Shane's grandfather tutors him: "Real estate always bounced back. It's like Spaldeens."

Dune Road
Quogue
July 19

Dear Lenny,

I'm sending a copy of this letter and the
enclosed to Jerry. Obviously, it is the
barest of skeletons - but is on the line
we worked out and agreed on. And will, I
hope, be some sort of basis for all of us
to do some thinking on before we meet again.

I don't know whether you've been so busy that
you've missed all the juvenile gang war news.
Not only is it all over the papers everyday,
but it is going to be all over the movie
screens. Arthur Miller, or so I read, is doing
an original drama on the subject for movies.

By accident, then, we have hit on an idea which
is suddenly extremely topical, timely, and just
plain hot. For this reason, I hope we can get
to serious work on it as early as we planned.
But more than that, if there is any way of getting the thing done this season, I hope we can
find it. To my way of thinking, it would be
perfect timing to present this on Broadway
early in the Spring. I don't know if it's possible
but with all this splurge of interest in the subject, I think we would be missing a big opportunity
if we didn't capitalize on it.

Incidentally, I hope you noticed I didn't say
"East Side Story." This was because of our
mutual feeling that the locale should not be
specific or definitely placed in any specific
city.

Love to Felicia, your brood and yourself,

·71·

"East Side Story"

Crossing Delancey

In retrospect, it sounds like a bad joke: Let's put on a show, a musical version of *Romeo and Juliet* that takes place in Manhattan. Recruit Leonard Bernstein to compose the music, Arthur Laurents to write the book, Jerome Robbins to direct the choreography. The young ill-fated lovers, a Jewish girl and an Italian Catholic boy. Call the play *East Side Story.*

That was 1949. Six years later, New York's demographics had begun to shift so profoundly that the plot was transplanted uptown to a neighborhood known as Lincoln Square. *West Side Story* was born.

By the 1950s, the heavily Jewish Lower East Side and adjacent Little Italy were morphing into neighborhoods that would not have been recognizable when the century began. The East Village was emerging as a separate enclave, heavily Hispanic. Chinatown was encroaching from the south. Whites—Italians and Jews both—were fleeing to Brooklyn and Queens or, better yet, to the New York suburbs or retiring to air-conditioned comfort in Florida.

By 1955, Bernstein and Laurents were in Hollywood working on separate ventures when the *Romeo and Juliet* project was revived. "In Shakespeare," Laurents recalled, "the nature of the conflict between the two houses is never specified. We had begun with religion, but that was dropped into the roomy swimming pool of the Beverly Hills Hotel. Instead, the racial problems of Los Angeles led us to shift our play from the Lower East Side of New York to the Upper West Side, and the conflict to that between a Puerto Rican gang and a polymorphous self-styled 'American' gang." (Tony, the Romeo character, was played onstage by Larry Kert, who was born in Los Angeles, and in the film by Richard Beymer, who hailed from Iowa.)

The play opened in 1957, with lyrics by Stephen Sondheim in his Broadway debut. By the time the movie version opened four years later, the Upper West Side was undergoing changes that would transform it even more radically than the Lower East Side. By the 1950s, a largely Irish working-class neighborhood had become increasingly black and Puerto Rican (named San Juan Hill after the black soldiers who fought in the Spanish-American War) and was targeted by Robert Moses, the city's construction coordinator, as his largest urban renewal project. In 1955 he officially declared the neighborhood an expendable slum and condemned the property. Residents challenged the designation but lost in the United States Supreme Court. In 1958 more than sixteen thousand were relocated.

Slum clearance was delayed to accommodate exterior photography for the film. The full completion of Lincoln Center for the Performing Arts in 1969, along with construction of Fordham University's West Side campus and the Lincoln Towers housing complex, transformed San Juan Hill and laid the groundwork for a brand-new neighborhood that defied both the street grid and what had seemed like inevitable and irreversible urban decay.

The etymology of *West Side Story* is much better documented than that of Lincoln Square and its namesake, Lincoln Center. The name was bestowed on the area bounded by Columbus and Amsterdam Avenues and West Sixty-Third and Sixty-Sixth Streets by the Board of Aldermen in 1906, ironically, during the tenure of Mayor George B. McClellan, Jr., whose father ran for president against Lincoln. Fifty years later, as Sondheim's lyrics to West Side Story suggested, Lincoln Square was a very different place:

Immigrant goes to America,
Many hellos in America;
Nobody knows in America
Puerto Rico's in America!

· 72 ·

Ruiz Marathon Certificate

Runners-Up

Success has a thousand fathers, so the New York City Marathon will never be an orphan. Only 127 competitors ran the first marathon, which looped around Central Park in 1970 (55 runners finished). Forty years later, more than 45,000 runners were clocked passing the finish line. It is now the largest marathon in the world.

The race was first organized by the presidents of the New York Road Runners Club, Fred Lebow and Vincent Chiappetta. Gary Muhrcke won the first 26.2-mile marathon in 2:31:38. About a hundred spectators cheered him on. Since then, hundreds of thousands of runners have participated in the New York City Marathon, and millions of New Yorkers and hometown fans from around the world have lined the route. (In 2011 Geoffrey Mutai of Kenya broke the course record with 2:05:06.)

The marathon was a decidedly modest affair until 1976, when New York, deep in the fiscal dumps, was desperate for something to celebrate. Mayor Abraham D.

Beame and prominent civic boosters including the Rudin family, aggressively wooed the Democratic National Convention to New York as the nation celebrated its bicentennial. To mark the occasion, several New Yorkers suggested that the marathon be expanded to encompass all five boroughs. One was George Spitz, a

runner, state civil servant, and municipal gadfly. Another was Mortimer Matz, a genius at press agentry who suggested the route to Percy Sutton, the Manhattan borough president.

Sutton was instrumental in enlisting Beame and the Rudin family, and what

began as a onetime event to mark the bicentennial became an annual international celebration of the city's diversity as runners course through ethnic enclaves—from Orthodox Jews in Brooklyn to Dominicans in the South Bronx—and a driver of the city's recovery from its disheartening brush with bankruptcy in the mid-1970s.

The 1979 race was immortalized by Rosie Ruiz, a twenty-five-year-old office worker in a Manhattan commodities firm who won the women's division with a time of 2:56:29. It was later determined that Ruiz, who moved to the United States from Cuba with her family when she was four, took a sixteen-mile shortcut by subway—the modern equivalent, *Sports Illustrated* observed, "of Pheidippides riding a goat partway from Marathon to Athens."

In racing circles, Ruiz's stunt was scandalous. To ordinary New Yorkers, it was the stuff of legend. Appropriately enough, she said she hoped to become an actress.

NO STANDING

←→

EXCEPT VEHICLES WITH

CONSUL-C
DIPLOMAT-A&D

LICENSE PLATES

SP-231B   DEPT OF TRANSPORTATION

D/S DECALS ONLY

SP-699G   DEPT OF TRANSPORTATION

M-236	M-245
M-321	M-238
M-276	M-336
C-161	M-392
M-360	

· 73 ·

DPL Parking Sign

Becoming the Global Capital

If there was ever any doubt that New York was the world's capital, the city's global preeminence was validated in 1952 with the opening of the seventeen-acre United Nations headquarters complex on Manhattan's East Side.

New York officials were determined to court the UN in a selection process that lasted over a year. "Looking back," wrote Charlene Mires, a history professor at Rutgers University–Camden, "if it all seems a bit crazy, then we have lost touch with the atmosphere of determination, hope and anxiety that characterized American society at the end of the Second World War."

One faction wanted the complex to be in Geneva, Switzerland, at the former League of Nations headquarters. Boston, Philadelphia, and San Francisco were among 248 localities vying for the honor in the United States. Suburban hopes to host the headquarters were not helped when diplomats got lost on their way to the Rockefeller estate near Tarrytown, New York.

The UN met temporarily at the Sperry Corporation's headquarters in Lake Success on Long Island; at the old New York City Pavilion from the 1939 World's Fair in Flushing Meadows, Queens; and on the Bronx campus of Hunter College (now Lehman College). James J. Lyons, the borough president, crowed: "History will record that the Bronx was the first capital of the world."

Nelson Rockefeller negotiated on a napkin the purchase of the East Side site from William Zeckendorf, a prominent developer, for $8.5 million contributed by Nelson's father, John D. Rockefeller, Jr. The site, in the Turtle Bay section of Midtown East, now has extraterritorial status and is dominated by the thirty-nine-story Secretariat Building, a glass and marble vertical slab, and the domed General Assembly hall, which can seat eighteen hundred. Plans for the entire complex were overseen by Wallace K. Harrison, the favorite architect of the Rockefeller family, and proceeded from designs by Le Corbusier of France and Oscar Niemeyer of Brazil. (Today an expansion just south of the existing campus is planned.)

What began as an outgrowth of the Allied governments in World War II grew to include 193 permanent missions (the flags are flown in alphabetical order, in English) staffed by 35,000 diplomats. City officials estimate that the UN contributes $2.5 billion to New York's economy.

Any other city would be proud of its distinction as the world capital, but New Yorkers are typically blasé. Mentioning the United Nations conjures up comments about traffic congestion and challenges to parking, especially each fall, when the General Assembly convenes. Serial motorcades ferrying heads of state and the public outpourings in support of or opposition to one cause or another clog Manhattan streets. DPL vehicle license plates, once granted by New York, have been supplanted by State Department plates. The city insists that only 5 percent of the tickets issued to the city's nearly 2,500 diplomatic license-plate holders go unpaid.

Baseball

The Shot Heard 'Round the World

This is the only object among the 101 that does not exist.

Or, if it survives somewhere, over six decades since it disappeared, its whereabouts remain a mystery worthy of Judge Crater, the Manhattan jurist who disappeared in 1930 after leaving Billy Haas's Chophouse on West Forty-Fifth Street on his way to a comedy called *Dancing Partner* at the Belasco. It's one thing to be swallowed up, intentionally or not, in a faceless crowd in Times Square. It is another to vanish in front of thirty-four thousand eyewitnesses keenly interested in your fate.

The missing object is a baseball. Not just any baseball but the "shot heard 'round the world," as Pete Coutros, a *Daily News* caption writer, christened Bobby Thomson's decisive three-run homer, which won the National League pennant for the New York Giants on October 3, 1951. The bat survived, but not the ball.

It was an improbable finale to the cross-river rivalry against the Brooklyn Dodgers. As late as mid-August, the Dodgers were leading the Giants by thirteen and a half games. The three-game playoff series was tied, with the Dodgers leading 4 to 2 when the bottom of the ninth inning began.

Pitching in the first major sports contest broadcast coast-to-coast on television was Ralph Branca, off of whom Thompson had hit a two-run homer in the first game. Thompson smashed Branca's fastball into the stands. The Dodgers turned their backs—except for Jackie Robinson, who watched, hands on hips, to be certain that Thomson touched every base on his victory lap.

Fans swarmed the field, grabbing Thomson's cap and even tugging at his underwear. His bat and Branca's rosin bag wound up in the Hall of Fame in Cooperstown, New York, but the ball was never found. Brian Biegel, a documentarian, later claimed it was retrieved by an errant nun from Buffalo who died in 1990 and whose belongings, consigned to a shoe box, were subsequently discarded.

Controversy dogged the game after Joshua Prager, a *Wall Street Journal* reporter, discovered that the Giants used a telescope to regularly steal the opposing catcher's hand signals. (Thomson was aware of the sign-stealing but insisted he hadn't been tipped to Branca's fastball, and Branca graciously commented: "Even if Bobby knew what was coming, he had to hit it.")

The game's impact beyond baseball left no doubts. "I was not any longer a baseball fan," Arthur Miller wrote, "but when I heard what had happened I felt the axis of the world had shifted slightly." John Steinbeck weighed in with "Probably the best game I or anyone ever saw." In *Deconstructing Harry,* Woody Allen wrote: "The '51 Giants were the one genuine miracle of my lifetime. When he hit that home run, that was the only hint I've ever had that there may be a God." From death row on Sing Sing, atomic spy Julius Rosenberg wrote, "Gloom of gloom. The dear Dodgers lost the pennant."

The ball remains the stuff of legend. Vic Ziegel, a columnist and editor for the *New York Post* and the *Daily News,* dubbed it "the Holy Grail of sports."

·75·

Subway Token

Turnstile Justice

Today they've been relegated to collectors' items—dangling from charm bracelets ($190 for five tokens at the Transit Museum), decorating cuff links ($80) and chocolates ($8 for a box of 16). They turn up regularly in piggy banks and jars of old coins. Like Checker cabs and Spaldeens, they may seem like they've been around forever, but those familiar brass subway tokens date from only 1953.

They were introduced by the New York City Transit Authority when the fare was raised from 10 cents to 15. The reason was technological. Turnstiles could accept a nickel or a dime but not both. (The price had been artificially propped up at 5 cents for nearly a half century, until July 1, 1948.)

On July 22, 1953, 12 million tokens with the "Y" in "NYC" punched out and another 5 million solid ones went on sale. Eventually, 48 million small "Y" tokens were minted. The 15-cent fare lasted until 1966. Typically, but not always, fare increases were accompanied by new tokens. In 1970, a larger "Y" version was introduced when the fare rose to 30 cents. That token endured (about 50 million were stamped out) as the fare rose to 35 cents two years later and to 50 cents in 1975.

The subway celebrated its seventy-fifth anniversary in 1979 with a jubilee token that included a diamond-shaped hole. A large solid brass token was introduced in 1980, when the fare was raised to 60 cents. About 60 million were minted through 1985, as the fare rose to 75 cents and then to 90 cents. (Similar Connecticut Turnpike tokens cost one-third as much and illegally found their way into subway turnstiles until 1985, when the turnpike tolls were discontinued.)

In 1986 a bull's-eye token with a lighter-colored center was introduced, when a $1 fare was imposed. Eventually, 90 million were made. A slightly smaller token with a five-borough pentagonal hole was introduced in 1995, when the fare was increased to $1.50.

The token's gradual demise had been conceived in the 1980s and set in motion in 1994 but took nearly another decade to effectuate. After fifty years, tokens were phased out in 2003, replaced by the flexible plastic MetroCard. Transit officials estimate that 1.6 million of the original "Y" cutouts remain in warehouses (enough for 800,000 pairs of cuff links).

"Tokens will become cuff links and buttons and watches and who knows what else," Kenneth T. Jackson, the Columbia University historian, said presciently in 2003. "All that rummaging through your change, all that standing in line at the booth," he added. "Who needs it?"

Indeed, few New Yorkers objected when the Metropolitan Transportation Authority voted to phase out the tokens. Yet no object generated more nostalgia from *New York Times* readers. "When I was in high school," Diane Walsh of Miami remembered, "we would put them in our loafers instead of pennies so we would never get stranded somewhere without subway fare home."

·76·

The Checker

Taxis That Hurried

No other American city has a higher proportion of mass transit riders—nearly half of New Yorkers commute by subway or bus. Nor is any city as dependent on taxis. While only 1 percent of the 4.3 million New Yorkers who commute to work every day take a cab, in 2011 the city's nearly 13,000 yellow-medallion taxis made about 500,000 trips daily and carried a total of 240 million passengers (the peak was 246 million in 1999).

From 1952 to 1986, Checker Motors in Kalamazoo, Michigan, manufactured the A8/Marathon, distinguished by a horizontal checkerboard stripe. Thousands clogged New York streets in all colors until 1970, when city officials required that every cab available for street hails be painted yellow. The bulky Checkers, in particular, transformed Manhattan's broad avenues and cramped side streets into glacial mustard-colored rivulets.

A 1996 law requires taxis to be replaced every six years. No new Checkers have been made in over two decades. Moreover, none of the old ones meet the city's strict air pollution standards that apply to for-hire vehicles. The last Checker, with almost a million miles on its odometer, was retired in 1999. The Checkers were replaced mostly by Ford Crown Victorias.

In 2012, after a five-year process, the Nissan NV200 won a competition to become the "Taxi of Tomorrow." The boxy van, phased in beginning in 2013, looks more like the old Checker than like many modern passenger cars. The NV200 is powered by a four-cylinder engine and is designed to reduce carbon emissions and improve fuel efficiency. The cab has sliding doors (to prevent accidents with pedestrians, cyclists, or other vehicles), a transparent roof panel for greater visibility, independently controlled air-conditioning for passengers, side windows that open, overhead reading lights, a mobile charging electrical outlet, a navigation system, a flat, no-hump rear floor area, an intercom that connects the driver and the passenger, air bags, and a "low-annoyance" horn configured with exterior lights that display when the driver is honking.

During the Depression, when drivers outnumbered passengers, many owners could not afford to renew their medallions for the annual ten-dollar fee. In 2011, a medallion traded for $1 million. Hacking, in the traditional sense, remains a gateway job for immigrants. About nine in ten taxi drivers are immigrants, with Pakistan, Bangladesh, and India accounting for nearly four in ten. (The NV200 is also an immigrant, manufactured in Mexico.)

Taxis are typically the most expensive way of getting to work. The annual median cost for everyday commuters was $4,704, according to a recent survey by the city—over twice that of any other means of transportation (commuting by railroad—not subways—was the second most expensive). Ten times as many New Yorkers walk to work as take a taxi, which reminds Sam Schwartz, a traffic consultant, of an old joke: " 'Shall we walk or do we have time to take a taxi?' Those who can afford to commute by taxi," he said, "probably have the luxury of time on their side."

·77·

Cross Bronx Expressway

The Highwayman

Robert Moses enjoyed quoting Beardsley Ruml, an economist, statistician, Macy's executive, and father of the withholding tax: "If the ends don't justify the means," he liked to say, "what does?" Lillian Edelstein would have been more comfortable with a quotation from Harry Emerson Fosdick, the Protestant pastor whose brother ran the Rockefeller Foundation in the 1930s: "He who chooses the beginning of a road chooses the place it leads to. It is the means that determine the end."

There is no record that Lillian Edelstein ever met Jane Jacobs, but the two would have been united in their disdain for Moses and his bulldozer diplomacy. In a way, Lillian Edelstein's indefatigable opposition to Moses's proposed Cross Bronx Expressway in the early 1950s paved the way for Jacobs's unabashed urbanism and vigilante activism in the 1960s—advocacy that defeated the Power Broker and blocked his proposed Lower Manhattan Expressway, which would have bisected Greenwich Village and obliterated much of Washington Square Park.

An expressway across the Bronx had been suggested since the 1920s, to link the proposed George Washington Bridge with points east. The route posed enormous engineering challenges and required tunneling through solid rock. Moses's

plan called for crossing valleys and rerouting rivers for seven miles that intersected more than a hundred streets, subways, and commuter rail lines. Ernest Clark, the designer, was quoted as saying that "only a man like Mr. Moses would have the audacity to believe that one could push from one end of the Bronx to the other."

In an affidavit, Edelstein described herself as just "a Jewish housewife," which would be about as ingenuous as Moses calling himself merely an accomplished parks administrator. "I was a resident of 867 East 176th Street before the Cross-Bronx Expressway project forced my family and I out of our home," she wrote. What she lacked in grammar, she made up in gumption after she received a letter from Moses, as the city construction coordinator, December 4, 1952, informing her and her neighbors that they had ninety days to vacate their apartments or they would be evicted.

"I put everything I had into the fight for our neighborhood and homes but in the end, out efforts were no use against the immense power and control of Robert Moses over New York and its officials," declared Edelstein, who paid $56 a month rent for Apartment 2F (her husband, Sam, earned $75 a week making ladies' hats). "Moses ordered the demolition of 159 buildings housing 1,530 families instead of tearing down 6 buildings housing 19 families and the Third Avenue Transit Co. Bus Terminal."

Moses was, in a sense, bluffing. He did not yet hold title to Edelstein's apartment building or the others. Nonetheless, she recalled, the letter was "like the floor opened up underneath your feet." Rejecting any other route, Moses indiscriminately parted the East Tremont section of the South Bronx, hastening an exodus of white middle-class families that was already under way and might have been inevitable regardless.

Edelstein lost. But in galvanizing her East Tremont neighbors into their Alamo-like last stand, she put a human face on the polarizing upheaval wrought by an urban renewal philosophy that favored the suburbs over the city and highways over mass transit.

·78·

Cargo Container

Shipping Out

New York introduced a crewless subway train. A 114-day newspaper strike began. The Mets arrived. That same year, 1962, the Port Authority opened the world's first fully containerized port. Not in New York but in Elizabeth, New Jersey. Elizabeth would become the nation's container capital, while the original Port of New York—the cargo and passenger piers jutting into the harbor from Manhattan, Brooklyn, and Staten Island that had defined maritime New York for over three centuries—endured a precipitous decline from which they have never recovered. The waterfront would be transformed.

While New York was already blessed with a natural harbor, the Erie Canal, the regular departure of packet ships, and the triangular trade in cotton all figured in New York's ascendancy on the East Coast. Containerization had begun in Port Newark as early as 1955 by Sea Land, which integrated ocean shipping in containers that could be transferred onto trucks and rail lines. Access to the New Jersey Turnpike meant, as the Port Authority boasted, that a truck could travel from Port Newark to Chicago without stopping for a single traffic light.

As recently as the 1960s, a fifth of the nation's ocean-borne general cargo was shipped through the Port of New York. Within two decades, the share had plum-

meted to a tenth (although total tonnage was up). By the late 1980s, the last operating cargo pier in Manhattan (which handled nearly a billion bananas a year)
ceased operations. After more than fifty years, Dole Fresh Food Co. consolidated
its operations in Delaware, a departure from the Port of New York that represented the ultimate banana split. Even the South Street Seaport Museum struggled
to survive as a repository for past glory.

In a half century, the number of active registered longshoremen declined by 90
percent, to a little more than three thousand. While the overall cargo hauled
through the Port of New York *and* New Jersey soared, the vast bulk of it was
handled in the giant container ports in Elizabeth and Newark. A revival of ferries
and cruise ship traffic and the expansion of ocean liner berths in Brooklyn have
kept the New York side of the harbor alive, as do garbage scows, municipal waste-
treatment plant sludge boats, and lighters carrying fuel oil. But the maritime traffic
that symbolized the city—immigration to Castle Garden and Ellis Island, freight-
ers to Brooklyn and the Hudson and East River docks, and passenger liners to the
Hudson River piers—has faded into history. The waterfront is being retooled for
recreation and residential development.

The forty-foot-long steel shipping container, which replaced break bulk cargo
hoisted in nets, was not the only culprit behind the decline. However, containers
required acres of storage space that the piers in Manhattan and even Brooklyn
could not accommodate (the Maher terminal in Elizabeth alone is more than half
the size of Central Park). The shift suggests Joseph Schumpeter's paradigm of
capitalism's "creative destruction." Container facilities still operate in Red Hook,
Brooklyn, and Howland Hook, Staten Island. Overall, the port annually handles
more than three million containers, loaded and empty, the vast bulk of them in
New Jersey.

The bistate port is the nation's third largest (after Los Angeles and Long Beach,
California) and the largest on the East Coast, although oil prices pushed the port
of Houston past New York in 2012 as the nation's top export market. Harbor
channels are being deepened, and the Bayonne Bridge over Kill Van Kull, separat-
ing Staten Island from New Jersey, is being raised to accommodate the supercon-
tainer ships that will be able to navigate the Panama Canal.

• 79 •

Here's Johnny

Through a Lens, Darkly

Just as the anthological *Grand Central Station* symbolized New York for radio listeners from 1937 to 1954 ("the crossroads of a million private lives, a gigantic stage on which are played a thousand dramas daily"), *The Tonight Show* would define the city for television viewers in the 1960s and '70s. No TV host shaped the city's image beyond its borders more than Johnny Carson.

The first commercial television licenses were granted to CBS and NBC in New York in 1941, and the city immediately emerged as the nation's TV capital (just as it had in the early days of movies). On October 1, 1962, Groucho Marx introduced Carson, a thirty-seven-year-old former quiz show host, as Jack Paar's replacement on NBC. Greeted by thunderous applause, Marx deadpanned: "Boy, you'd think it was Vice President Nixon." In his first opening monologue, Carson kidded the Kennedys and chided Mississippi, but not New York.

Paar had transformed his Manhattan studio into Everyman's living room. For the first decade of his thirty-year reign, Carson transported viewers from their pillows or couches to a hip Manhattan nightclub and gingerly nudged the Big Apple's permissiveness onto network television (he once recalled when the censors would not even allow a "pause" to be described as pregnant).

By the 1960s, New York had awakened from the slumber of the Eisenhower years to spawn the twist at the Peppermint Lounge, to celebrate the city's global stature with another World's Fair, to revel in the Mets' unlikely World Series upset

and a Jets Super Bowl victory, and to briefly entertain the hope that John V. Lindsay, the telegenic successor to Mayor Robert F. Wagner (the taciturn and similarly undervalued local incarnation of Eisenhower), could succeed in a job that he cleverly dubbed the second toughest in America.

Carson's monologues about blackouts, daylight muggings, middle-of-the-night street repairs, and of course, cabbies ("Any time four New Yorkers get into a cab together without arguing, a bank robbery has just taken place") didn't diminish the city so much as validate its uniqueness.

On the show, Lindsay would join in, joking about never breathing air he couldn't see and about a computerized matchmaker in Central Park: When a young man described himself to the computer as sensitive and rich, the machine mugged him. Dazzled by his own stardom, Lindsay ran for president in 1972, only to discover that his popularity was skin-deep. A month after Lindsay quit the race, Carson decamped for California. "It was a migration that, along with the demise of *The Ed Sullivan Show* on CBS the year before," Frank Rich wrote in the *Times*, "marked the end of Manhattan's parity with Hollywood as a glitz capital for a national audience." Still, as Skitch Henderson, the *Tonight Show*'s musical director, recalled, "Hollywood was like chocolate syrup; it smothered you." The show returned to New York with Jimmy Fallon as host in 2014.

·80·

The Anthora

Our Cups Runneth Over

Long before Starbucks competed with national bank branches and chain drugstores for every retail rental corner, takeout coffee was invariably delivered briskly by countermen to New Yorkers in a blue-and-white cardboard coffee cup featuring a totemic Grecian vase.

A few years ago, *The New York Times* proclaimed the cup as "the most enduring piece of ephemera in New York City," as "vivid an emblem of the city as the Statue of Liberty, beloved of property masters who need to evoke Gotham at a glance in films and on television." (Without the iconic cup, the *Times* wrote, "*Law & Order* could scarcely exist.") It evoked the city to the rest of the world. No other artifact of its size said New York as definitively as the Anthora.

Enshrined in museums and inspiring myriad imitations and even hefty ceramic versions, the cup was designed by Leslie Buck, a refugee from a concentration camp in Nazi Europe, who started a paper cup company with his brother in the late 1950s in Mount Vernon, New York. He never trained as an artist but drew the pervasive design himself in the 1960s, as sales manager for the Sherri Cup Co. in Kensington, Connecticut, which was trying to crack the New York market.

Hundreds of millions of the cups were manufactured annually, most of them destined for ubiquitous Greek-owned diners, delicatessens, and vendors from street-corner carts (and later, to formerly Italian-operated pizzerias, in another example of ethnic succession) in the metropolitan area.

For obscure reasons, possibly derived from Buck's Eastern European accent (he was born in what was then Czechoslovakia and now is Ukraine), the amphora—a large vase or urn—depicted in the Greek national colors was called the Anthora. Ringed by a white meander above and below, in classical lettering, it featured a motto that, the *Times* wrote, offered "welcome intimations of tenderness, succor and humility" in six mostly monosyllabic words: "We Are Happy To Serve You." The cup was its own advertisement.

The cups were emblematic of the ethnic commercial dominance in various job categories in the city, as one group or another gravitated toward fellow immigrants who had paved the way. No coincidence that there were disproportionate numbers of Irish cops; Jewish tailors; Italian barbers, shoeshine boys, and sanitation men; South Asian newsdealers; Filipino nurses; Irish and Italian longshoremen; German brewers; Latin American gardeners; and Afghan and Bangladeshi food cart vendors.

Demand for the distinctive design declined as new immigrant groups, including Koreans, succeeded Greek restaurateurs. Instead of staffing delis before dawn and on weekends, the second- or third-generation Greek-Americans moved to the suburbs and graduated into the professions.

Sherri, which manufactured five hundred million cups annually as recently as two decades ago, was selling fewer than half that number by 2005 through Solo Cup Co., which absorbed it. Solo now makes the cup only on request, while other companies still offer distinctly Greek—if anachronistic—variations, including columns or a discus thrower, on Leslie Buck's original and durable design.

·81·

Night

Razing Hell

Beavers, flour barrels, a windmill, a sailor, and an Indian adorn the city's official seal, but what more fitting symbol for the City of New York than a wrecking ball? Little of the Dutch heritage survives, and even the 1700 City Hall, where George Washington was inaugurated as the young nation's first president, was razed and sold for scrap.

But no single edifice exemplified New York's indifference to its past more than the old Pennsylvania Station, commissioned in Midtown West as the railroad's belated portal to Manhattan by Alexander Cassatt, the Pennsy's president, whose sister, Mary, was the famous impressionist artist featured at the 1913 Armory Show.

The granite gateway gave the Pennsylvania Railroad a Manhattan foothold, but as one wag noted, it reduced New York to a two-minute stop on the line from Rahway, New Jersey, to Long Island City. Consisting of nine acres of marble, the station opened in 1910 on two superblocks, flanked by West Thirty-First and Thirty-Third Streets and Seventh and Eighth Avenues, just three years ahead of Grand Central Terminal. Grand Central would prove to be not only more enduring but also more transformative. By decking over dozens of acres of open-air tracks

to create Park Avenue and by leveraging air rights over the newly created real estate to monetize its investment, Grand Central accomplished a goal that McKim, Mead & White's Penn Station never could: It shifted Manhattan's cultural center of gravity, delivering the heart of midtown to the doorstep of a station that, when an earlier Grand Central opened on East Forty-Second Street in 1871, had been demeaned as neither particularly grand nor central.

Penn Station would survive for only fifty-three years, but it would not die in vain. The wanton demolition, so developers could replace the majestic head house and train shed—modeled on the Baths of Caracalla—with the latest banal incarnation of Madison Square Garden and an even blander office building, provoked a backlash that led to the creation of a city Landmarks Preservation Commission. Its legal authority, after a subsequent campaign to save Grand Central from the same ignoble fate, was validated by the United States Supreme Court in 1978. Grand Central celebrated its centennial in 2013.

A newly constituted station, named for former senator Daniel Patrick Moynihan to be installed in the former General Post Office across Eighth Avenue from Penn Station, may still be in the offing. Meanwhile, commuters on the Long Island Rail Road, Amtrak, and New Jersey Transit can only imagine the majestic concourse that met the wrecking ball beginning on October 28, 1963 (with the removal of the first eagle of a conclave of twenty-two). "One entered the city like a god," wrote Vincent Scully, the Yale architectural historian. "One scuttles in now like a rat."

Penn Station's monumental columns were recycled as landfill in the New Jersey Meadowlands, and so was *Day*, one of Adolph A. Weinman's allegorical sculptures, a gentle marble maiden—modeled on the ubiquitous Audrey Munson (*Civic Fame*)—and adorned in silken robes, a sunflower garland, and a bayberry wreath. "Has the city been sacked?" Moynihan demanded after seeing Eddie Hausner's 1968 photograph of the ruined sculpture in *The New York Times*.

Four pairs of *Day* and *Night* flanked clocks on the station's granite facades. Weinman's eleven-foot-high pink Tennessee marble *Night* survives in the sculpture garden of the Brooklyn Museum. Clutching a drooping poppy, she was donated by the Lipsett Demolition Co., which won the contract to raze Penn Station.

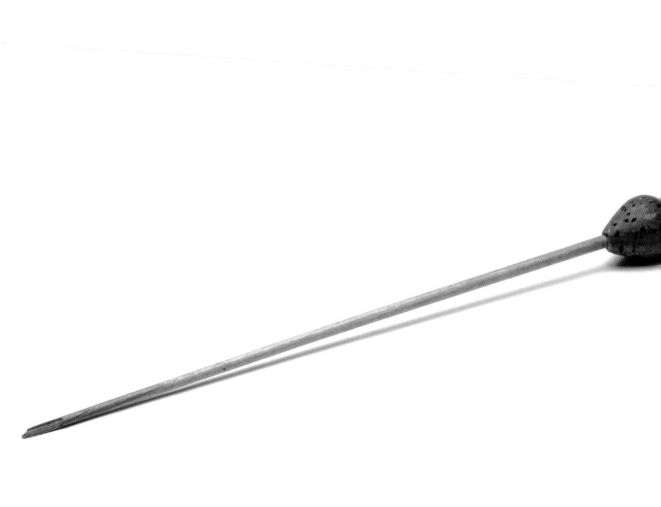

·82·

Bernstein's Baton

The Music Man

On April 2, 1842, the grandson of a fife player in the Continental Army gathered local musicians and organized the New York Philharmonic Society. Ureli Corelli Hill not only founded the society but was also named president, and later that year, he inaugurated its concert series by conducting Beethoven's Fifth Symphony at the Apollo Rooms on lower Broadway. By 2010, the orchestra had given its fifteen thousandth concert, a global record that more than validated its status as the oldest symphony orchestra in America.

Since 1842, it has commissioned or premiered works such as Antonín Dvořák's symphony *From the New World* and Aaron Copland's *Connotations;* inaugurated regular radio broadcasts in 1922 and its Young People's Concerts in 1924; and performed in more than 430 cities in more than sixty countries on five continents, including in Hanoi, Vietnam, and Pyongyang in the Democratic People's Republic of Korea, the first visit there by any American orchestra. (Like the Philharmonic, the Metropolitan Opera, which also has performed at Lincoln Center since 1966, is a global brand. The Met was founded in 1883 and opened its first opera house on Broadway and Thirty-Ninth Street.)

The orchestra fared better than its founder, whose musical and personal trajectory slid downhill. While the Philharmonic thrived, Hill invented a piano that never had to be tuned (it used bells instead of strings), but he never marketed it successfully, lost money on land investments in New Jersey, and because of age, was forced into retirement as a violinist. At seventy-three, he took his own life, leaving a note that asked: "Why should or how can a man exist and be powerless to earn means for his family?"

Subsequent presidents of the Philharmonic have included such civic luminaries as George Templeton Strong, Andrew Carnegie, and Oswald Garrison Villard. The composers and conductors who led the orchestra included Antonín Dvořák, Gustav Mahler, Richard Strauss, Arturo Toscanini, Igor Stravinsky, Aaron Copland, Bruno Walter, George Szell, Erich Leinsdorf, and Leonard Bernstein.

Like so many New Yorkers, Bernstein was born somewhere else: in Lawrence, Massachusetts, in 1918. After graduating from Harvard, he was named assistant conductor of the New York Philharmonic in 1943 (at age twenty-five) and made his conducting debut with the Philharmonic as a last-minute replacement for the ailing Bruno Walter at a concert that was broadcast nationally on radio on November 14, 1943. He was named music director in 1958 and, in the next eleven years, would conduct more Philharmonic concerts than any of his predecessors. Bernstein was appointed laureate conductor after his farewell concert with the Philharmonic on May 17, 1969. He introduced millions of young people to music through special concerts and was famed as both conductor and composer. Bernstein collaborated with Betty Comden and Adolph Green on the 1944 show *On the Town,* wrote the score for the 1954 film *On the Waterfront* and teamed with Jerome Robbins, Stephen Sondheim, and Arthur Laurents on the Broadway musical and film versions of *West Side Story.*

In his farewell concert, Bernstein conducted Mahler's Third Symphony with a favorite baton, uniquely designed with a ball-shaped cork bottom that allowed him to fling his arms characteristically without losing his grip.

· 83 ·

Met Button

Art for Art's Sake

Talk about being worth the price of admission. For forty-two years, paid visitors to the Metropolitan Museum of Art identified themselves with circular metal buttons that found their way as artistic totems into the reliquary of New York. They came in sixteen colors and were ordered several times a year from Krays & Sons in Chelsea 1.6 million at a time, which is almost as many pieces of art as are in the Met's entire collection.

Sometimes confused by name with the Metropolitan Opera (but never with the baseball team of the same derivation), the Met occupies a special place in that constellation of museums, concert halls, theaters, publishing houses, studios, galleries, and digital start-ups and stalwarts that have elevated and validated New York as the nation's cultural capital. An estimated five million people visit the Met's sprawling exhibition halls on Fifth Avenue annually, making it the city's single most popular attraction. (One measure of its popularity are the peanut and ice cream vendors who, until a few years ago when competitors moved in, were paying the city $575,000-a-year to park two pushcarts at the foot of the museum's monumental outdoor staircase.)

Galvanized by John Jay, a lawyer and grandson of the Founding Father, and the

Union League Club, fellow civic leaders, art aficionados, and philanthropists incorporated the Metropolitan Museum of Art in 1870. Its first acquisition was an early-third-century Roman marble sarcophagus—apparently unsold by its maker and unused—found a few years earlier in what is now Turkey, a gift from the American vice consul. The museum moved to its current site a decade later. The original building, designed by Calvert Vaux and Jacob Wrey Mould, is completely surrounded by various additions and renovations that provide two million square feet of space. Today its two million pieces (tens of thousands of which are exhib-

ited at any given time) include the largest collection of Egyptian art outside of Cairo, twenty-five hundred European paintings, and impressive collections of art and ephemera ranging from armor to musical instruments and baseball cards. The Met has more wings than a cluster of dragonflies.

Under the Met's agreement with New York City (it stands on city-owned land), admission is technically free. But in 1970 the museum began strongly "suggesting" an admission charge (now twenty-five dollars). Originally, cumbersome paper tickets were used to identify paying customers, then dangerously sharp stickpins. Finally, the museum opted in 1971 for the one-inch metal button known as a lithotab, which has been reproduced in 550 different tints, most recently emblazoned with the ornate letter "M" as designed by Leonardo Da Vinci and adopted by the museum as its logo. The exhibition of artifacts from King Tut's tomb in the late 1970s merited a special design.

Ji Eon Kang, a student at the Parsons School of Design, created a silk and metal dress from admission buttons that is in the Costume Collection of the Met.

Citing the cost (the supplier sold them wholesale for $15.39 per thousand as recently as 2005, but the price had doubled), the Met discontinued the tin-plate buttons in 2013 and replaced them with detachable stickers.

·84·

Graffiti

The Handwriting on the Wall

T he words of the prophets are written on the subway walls, and the tenement halls," Paul Simon wrote. Also on the doors and facades of inhabited and derelict tenements, construction barriers, public monuments, and even vehicles (strikingly, only commercial ones)—virtually any blank surface provided an inviting canvas for what some people held up as incandescent vernacular art and others denounced as incendiary vandalism.

The "No Radio" signs directing thieves to someone else's car in the 1970s, then the crack vials in the 1980s, testified to the city's debasement. Motorists and even mass transit riders might overlook them. But New Yorkers could not avert their eyes from the proliferation of graffiti, a ubiquitous visual reminder (no matter how romanticized it was—"when it looked as if grafitti would take over the world." Norman Mailer wrote) that the inmates had taken over the asylum. The silent echo of graffiti, Mailer continued, was "the vibration of the profound discomfort it arouses, as if the unheard music of its proclamation and/or its mess, the rapt intent seething of its foliage, is the herald of some oncoming apocalypse less and less far away."

Whether graffiti was a cause or a product of urban decay, it became evidence of the "broken window theory" of crime. Only by removing it immediately would the urban apocalypse, whatever form it was to take, be forestalled. Subway cars—psychedelic moving murals—were the prime target. Riders felt confined enough without the windows being smeared with spray paint. But the graffiti contained no messages, political or sexual. Just names (sometimes with identifying street numbers). No more need be said about the perpetrators. "The sense that all are part of one world of uncontrollable predators seems inescapable," Harvard sociologist Nathan Glazer wrote. "It contributes to a prevailing sense of the incapacity of government, the uncontrollability of youthful criminal behavior and a resultant uneasiness and fear."

Most of the damage was done in unguarded subway-car storage yards, so Mayor Edward I. Koch persuaded transit police to patrol with German shepherds—he insisted on referring to them as "wolves"—inside rows of razor wire. Laws were passed to curtail the purchase of spray paint and even felt-tip pens. Entire neighborhoods were practically wiped clean. As the city began to revive in the mid-1990s, terms like "graffiti" and "squeegee men" grew anachronistic, just as "juvenile delinquency" or "ghetto" had become outdated in generations before. To find graffiti, you almost had to go to a gallery or a museum.

·85·

CBGB Sign

Rock and a Hard Place

From its earliest days, Greenwich Village was home to the city's outliers, New Yorkers who, for one reason or another, were escaping or exiled from the teeming, pestilent, Tory- or boss-controlled, and buttoned-down tip of downtown Manhattan to what would become known as the "Left Bank of America."

Which has prompted more than one critic to ask how this small, vaguely defined neighborhood, once an actual village beyond the city limits, came to play such an outsize role in Western culture and counterculture—a role epitomized by several legendary coffeehouses and clubs.

One was called Café Society, a term coined by Clare Booth Luce, the journalist, socialite, and, later, congresswoman. In 1938 Barney Josephson, a New Jersey shoe salesman and jazz aficionado, hijacked the term to mock her vision of New York's elitist nightclub scene. Just in case anyone didn't get the joke, he dubbed his cabaret—in the basement of a century-old building on Sheridan Square—"the wrong place for the Right people." ("Right" was capitalized, in what was perceived as another jab at sanctimonious conservatives.) "I wanted a club where blacks and whites worked together behind the footlights and sat together out front, a club whose stated advertised policy would be just that," he said. "There wasn't, so far as I know, a place like that in New York, or in the whole country, for that matter."

Josephson created a cultural phenomenon that promoted Billie Holiday, Alberta Hunter, Lena Horne, Sarah Vaughan, Big Joe Turner, Art Tatum, Mary Lou Williams, Jack Gilford, Zero Mostel, Imogene Coca, Carol Channing, and more. Among the rest was Abel Meeropol, who, with his wife, would adopt the sons of the convicted spies Ethel and Julius Rosenberg. Meeropol (writing under the name

Lewis Allan) came one day to deliver a new song, "Strange Fruit," a doleful protest of lynchings in the South.

Ultimately, the political cabaret was undone by politics. In 1947, after Josephson's brother Leon, a Communist, refused to testify before the House Un-American Activities Committee, the café owner was pummeled by prominent columnists. Customers left and the club was sold. "I think Barney and his story should be made into a movie," said Art D'Lugoff, the former owner of the Village Gate. "I think Café Society should be the story that should be told about our century."

D'Lugoff opened the Village Gate at Thompson and Bleecker in the first floor of a former flophouse in 1958. Until it closed in 1993, it featured marquee names like Dave Brubeck, Nina Simone, Aretha Franklin, and the long-running show *Jacques Brel Is Alive and Well and Living in Paris.* The ground floor is now a chain-store pharmacy.

CBGB was founded in 1973 on the Bowery, an original New York entertainment venue, by Hilly Kristal (he had owned another bar at the site since 1969) that aficionados knew by its full name, a mouthful: CBGB & OMFUG, which stood for Country Blue Grass Blues and Other Music for Uplifting Gormandizers. The club closed in 2006, replaced by a fashionable men's store. The awning survives at the Rock and Roll Hall of Fame.

The Gaslight was another fixture along with folk and comedy clubs that featured newcomers including Bob Dylan; Lenny Bruce; Woody Allen; and Peter, Paul, and Mary.

John Strausbaugh, a journalist, lamented recently that the Village has morphed into more "a place of recreation than creation, more occupied with preserving history than making it." Making culture and making a living are rarely compatible. He acknowledges one constant: "Complaining about newcomers and change is a long tradition in the Village."

·86·

Saturday Night Special

The Killing Fields

Public anxiety over what was termed juvenile delinquency in the 1950s and '60s (such as graffiti) seems almost quaint in comparison with the randomness, brutality, and breadth of crime in the 1970s and '80s. Geoffrey Canada, head of the Harlem Children's Zone, neatly capsulized the escalation in the title of his memoir, *Fist Stick Knife Gun: A Personal History of Violence.* Demographies had something to do with it. So did the shrinking police force, a direct consequence of the city's brush with bankruptcy in the mid-1970s. The crime wave was exacerbated by two striking external developments: the proliferation of cheap handguns, known as Saturday Night Specials, and the availability of a cheap form of cocaine called crack.

As many as 750,000 cut-rate handguns were flooding the United States annually from abroad, until import laws were tightened in 1968, spawning a cottage industry that produced millions of pot-metal weapons sold for as little as five dollars and were typically brandished in booze-fueled weekend domestic disputes. The weapons became emblematic of wanton violence, which peaked in the city in 1990, when 2,245 murders were recorded.

Along with the guns, few objects better symbolized a city out of control than the crack vials that contained a smokable and heavily addictive form of crystalline cocaine. Police Commissioner Benjamin Ward warned about it in the mid-1980s: "I have just been in California, where they have a new drug called 'rock' made from cocaine and very dangerous," he said. "When this drug hits New York it will undo all the progress we have made in bringing crime rates down."

The availability of crack triggered a wave of street crime that lasted a decade. Stiffer penalties for possession of the drug were sending a disproportionate number of poorer black and Hispanic buyers and sellers to prison. Within two decades, the devastation wrought by crack proved sobering to the next generation of potential drug users. The city's aggressive stop-and-frisk strategy discouraged some unknown number of would-be gun toters from brandishing their weapons in public. And as crime plummeted (including auto thefts, much less car radios), the city rebounded in the twenty-first century.

·87·

"Drop Dead"

The Headline That Drove Out a Ford

Mike O'Neill and Bill Brink returned from lunch on October 29, 1975, with a single question: Had President Gerald Ford agreed to bail out New York from its fiscal crisis? O'Neill was editor in chief of the New York *Daily News,* then the nation's largest-circulation newspaper (nearly two million copies sold daily, three million on Sundays). Brink was the managing editor.

"The people of this country will not be stampeded," Ford said in a speech that day at the National Press Club in Washington. "They will not panic when a few desperate New York officials and bankers try to scare New York's mortgage payments out of them." He vowed to veto any legislation that called for a bailout of the beleaguered city.

"Well, F.U.," O'Neill said in as many words, shaking his head. To which Brink replied with a glint in his eye, "Drop dead." That's how "Ford to City: Drop Dead" emerged as one of the nation's most famous newspaper headlines. It not only further endeared the *Daily News* to its loyal working-class readers; it helped cost Ford the election the following fall. He narrowly lost New York to Jimmy Carter, who vowed at Madison Square Garden, where he won the Democratic nomination in 1976, that he would never let New York City drop dead.

"It was a doozy of a speech, but events caught both sides by surprise," David Gergen, Ford's press secretary, remembered. "New Yorkers had not foreseen how tough the president would be, and Republicans in Washington had not anticipated how angry the response would be."

Ford's speech was another nadir in the city's roller-coaster brush with bank-

ruptcy. Two weeks earlier, on Friday, October 17, 1975, Mayor Abraham D. Beame had signed a formal petition attesting to municipal default. The police commandeered squad cars, poised to serve legal papers on banks that were the city's leading creditors. A court order signed by Justice Irving Saypol was pending to preserve the city government's assets. "I have been advised by the comptroller," a two-and-a-half-page mayoral news release began, "that the City of New York has insufficient cash on hand to meet debt obligations due today. This constitutes the default that we have struggled to avoid."

That signed petition was never invoked. Today it hangs framed in the Fifth Avenue office of Ira M. Millstein, one of the city's private lawyers during the fiscal crisis—a testament to the New Yorkers who, after meeting for hours in an Upper East Side apartment that October morning, dodged the financial fate that Detroit would suffer in 2013. In another near-miss, Albert Shanker, the teachers' union president, agreed to invest $150 million from his members' pension funds in city securities. Outside monitors were imposed on the city. "In the end," said Stephen Berger, the first director of the state Emergency Financial Control Board, "all the stuff we did was to keep the kid from drowning and three years later the economy swept him back on shore." Only two months after saying or meaning or merely implying "drop dead"—or perhaps after holding the city's feet to the fire—Ford signed legislation to provide federal loans to the city, which were repaid with interest. Governor Hugh L. Carey argued that Ford's public recalcitrance bought time for the city to make its case to an even more reluctant Congress, spurring New York's civic, business, and labor leaders to rally bankers in the United States and abroad (who feared their own investments would be harmed if New York defaulted on its debt), and to make the sacrifices that, only a few months before, the protagonists in the fiscal crisis had sworn they would never accept.

Luckily, said Richard Ravitch, one of the outside businessmen Carey enlisted, "we had a governor with a lot of balls and a lot of brains and a president who did what he had to do at the right time."

I Love New York

Have a Heart

A rebus may sound like something you ride back and forth crosstown, but in fact, it's a symbolic device that substitutes pictures for words. Milton Glaser has been a graphic designer for over sixty years, and nothing he conjured up became as popular as his logo for the "I Love New York" campaign when New York's name was mud.

Glaser once defined design as "moving an existing condition to a preferred one." Virtually any condition would have been preferable to the one that Governor Hugh L. Carey inherited in 1975 from his Republican predecessors—a state Urban Development Corp. veering off a fiscal cliff and a city—New York, no less—teetering on the brink of default.

If the nation's 1976 bicentennial celebration and the Democratic National Convention in New York provided a brief respite, the next year turned out to be even worse: The slash-and-burn fallout from the fiscal crisis began to be felt in neighborhoods all over, while the city plunged into a nightmare convergence of blackouts, a serial killer's shooting spree, a polarizing mayoral campaign, terrorist bombs linked to Puerto Rican nationalists, and a dysfunctional Bronx family known as the Yankees.

Glaser's assignment from Bill Doyle, the state assistant commerce commissioner, was to alter that existing chaotic condition, or at least the perception of it. Glaser outdid himself. A 1954 graduate of Cooper Union, he cofounded Push Pin Studios with his fellow alumni Seymour Chwast, Reynold Ruffins, and Edward Sorel. In 1968 he created *New York* magazine with Clay Felker. In his memoir, *Art Is Work,* he recalled that in 1975 "New York was perceived as a crime ridden, unfriendly if not hostile location, and the campaign using the phrase 'I Love New York' was intended to change the perception." Glaser sought "a visual equivalent for the words" and initially came up with a typographic solution—two lozenges atop each other reading simply "I Love" and "New York"—and it was approved. A week later, he wrote, "I was doodling in a cab and another idea suggested itself. I called Doyle and said, 'I have a better idea.'

"Forget it,' he said. 'Do you know how complicated it would be to get everyone together to approve it again?'

"'Let me show it to you,' I implored. He came down to the office, nodded, took away the new sketch, called a meeting and had it approved."

The red heart logo was first used in 1977. "It has been called with some hyperbole the most frequently replicated piece of printed ephemera of the century," Glaser says. "It is true that it has become so much a part of the general language that it's hard to imagine that it was actually designed by someone and did not always exist." The original design is part of the permanent collection of the Museum of Modern Art. The New York State Empire Development Corp. holds the copyright.

·89·

Pooper-Scooper

If You Want a Friend . . .

New York's garbage woes can be traced as far back as the mid-seventeenth century. First, trash was banned from the streets. Then, feral pigs were no longer allowed to roam free to forage on municipal thoroughfares. New Yorkers were forbidden to deposit "offensive animal matter" on public property, but that prohibition was wholesale in nature, targeted at slaughterhouses and rendering plants and at owners of the thousands of workhorses that died or were left for dead on city streets.

The "White Wings"—the spotless uniformed corps of sanitary engineers organized by George Waring, a former Civil War colonel, who roamed the city armed with brooms, shovels, and garbage cans on wheels—made a profound difference at the end of the nineteenth century. (Their helmets conveyed authority, their white uniforms, hygiene.) During the Depression, New Yorkers were required to curb their dogs, a campaign doomed by traffic, parked cars, lack of enforcement, and the city's own failure to sweep the streets.

After centuries of sidestepping the issue, New Yorkers tiptoed into a brave new world on August 1, 1978, when Health Law 1310 took effect. The law was not merely sanitary in tone. It was salutary, aimed at reweaving the city's tattered social fabric and proving once and for all that in at least one tangible way, New York

would be governable again. For the first time, New Yorkers were required by law to *pick up* after their pets—a daily deposit estimated at 250,000 pounds of feces in public places.

For all our New York exceptionalism, the law apparently was inspired by a local ordinance directed at a Great Dane in suburban Nutley, New Jersey. With prodding from the Lindsay administration, New Yorkers "were among the first people in the world to bend over and bag the unspeakable," Michael Brandow wrote in *New York's Poop Scoop Law*. Mayor Edward Koch, who inherited the role of chief enforcer of the new law, pithily expressed the prevailing popular sentiment: "I don't care if it's good luck to step in it. I don't want to."

Peer pressure coupled with potential punishment worked (better than the pet licensing law, which owners of about one in five of the half million or so dogs in the city comply with). In its own small way, the law, which barred owners from allowing their pets to "commit a nuisance" on a sidewalk of any public place, was a first step in redefining deviancy at a higher standard. New Yorkers improvised with recycled plastic bags and mass-produced long-handled Pooper-Scooper devices. The law was a model for subsequent campaigns to modify public behavior regarding smoking, buckling seat belts, and using condoms.

"I've been traveling these sidewalks for 25 years," Brandow wrote, "and know of no other aspect of urban life that manages to summon this sort of response. Not the sight of a little old lady being mugged, a child being molested, or a dog being beaten—nothing seems to hold the key to making New Yorkers stop whatever they're doing and 'get involved' like this does."

In Washington, Harry Truman memorably said, "If you want a friend, get a dog." In his later years, Ed Koch acknowledged that without a spouse or children, he was occasionally a little lonely. Why not get a dog? he was asked. "I wouldn't want to have to pick up after him," Koch replied.

·90·
Bullion

All That Glitters

I came to New York because I heard the streets were paved with gold," the legendary nineteenth-century immigrant lament began. "When I got here, I learned three things: The streets are not paved with gold. They are not paved at all. I am expected to pave them." Today New York's streets are more or less paved. They serve not only as heavily traversed thoroughfares for vehicles and pedestrians but also as canopies over chasmic trenches and tunnels gouged for subways, sewers, and utility conduits. What most New Yorkers don't realize is that while the streets are paved mostly with asphalt, there's more gold beneath them than any other place on earth.

There's gold in them thar basements, a lot more than is held in Fort Knox. The impregnable, fortress-like Federal Reserve Bank of New York Building on Liberty Street downtown contains the biggest known trove of monetary gold in the world, validating the city's preeminence as an international financial center. When the rusticated limestone and sandstone Florentine-style palazzo was completed in 1924, it was the largest bank building in the world.

All the gold stored there is owned by governments and international organizations. It amounts to what is estimated at more than one in twenty ounces of all the gold refined in human history. Storage began when the building opened in the early 1920s, but accelerated in the post–World War II period of global uncertainty and the search for safe havens. At its peak (in 1973, when the United States said foreign governments could no longer convert dollars into gold), the vaults—sitting on bedrock eighty feet below street level—held over 12,000 tons. Today the stash averages about 530,000 gold bars weighing 7,000 tons. (Fort Knox, the U.S. Bullion Depository in Kentucky, which opened in 1937 after the government banned private holdings of monetary gold, holds under 5,000 tons).

The gold is not fungible. Deposits are kept separately in 122 compartments, each numbered (not named) and secured with a padlock and two combination locks. Storage is free, but the Fed charges a fee of $1.25 each time a bar of gold is transferred. The bars themselves are trapezoidal or rectangular, depending on where they were cast (New York Assay Office bars have square corners, for example) and contain some copper, silver, or platinum to make them less malleable and easier to store. The vault itself, thirty feet below sea level, is airtight and watertight, sealed by a ninety-ton, nine-foot-tall cylinder surrounded by a 140-ton steel and concrete frame.

The Fed conducts public tours of its gold vault, which has figured in films (it starred in the 1995 Bruce Willis movie *Die Hard with a Vengeance*). The Fed isn't the only gold depository in New York City, although most of the others are much more circumspect about their holdings. Among the biggest—which store gold for the New York Mercantile Exchange—are Brink's, JPMorgan Chase, and HSBC Bank. On West Thirty-Ninth Street, near Bryant Park, there is no name to identify the building, only the nondescript address on the entrance to an HSBC depository. The doorway adjoins a tightly shuttered truck bay. Five security cameras peer down on passersby. When asked what was inside, a guard in the tiny lobby replied, "Just offices."

·91·

AIDS Button

An Epidemic's Grim Legacy

In 1982, 752 cases of a mysterious and fatal illness that would be called Acquired Immune Deficiency Syndrome were reported in New York City. By 2010, nearly 170,000 cases had been diagnosed. Over thirty years, the illness devastated whole communities and decimated professions such as fashion and the arts. At the same time, the disease served as a focal point for the gay rights movement, especially a group called ACT UP, which campaigned aggressively against the government's slow response to the epidemic.

As the New-York Historical Society recalled recently, "For those who lost partners, children, siblings, parents, and friends to HIV/AIDS in the later years of the 20th century, the memory of grief, fear, and mystery which pervaded New York at the beginning of the epidemic remains vivid. But for many New Yorkers and others today, this early period from 1981 to 1985 is virtually unknown. The activist movements that changed the nation's approach to catastrophic disease have overshadowed the panic of this period when a new and fatal enemy to public health was in its earliest stages and no one knew how to combat it." Edward Rothstein wrote in *The New York Times* that the society's exhibit recalls a time when, unlike some previous epidemics, "a disease seemed to burrow deeper than

mere death, transforming a city." The exhibition begins with images of the exuberant sexuality of the 1970s, including photos from Plato's Retreat (a sex club of the period) and of the male sunbathing pickup scene on Manhattan's West Side. One doctor, cited in accompanying text, recalled, "It was party time for everyone, heterosexuals as well as homosexuals. Then came disease." Rothstein wrote: "So, among a group that had only recently begun to taste the possibilities of openness, including some who had indulged in that freedom with abandon, there came this disease that assaulted that very way of life, attacking not just the body but the core of a nascent identity—and ultimately challenged sexual license."

ACT UP was founded by playwright Larry Kramer to raise awareness about the disease and the discrimination that gay people suffered. (As the Historical Society notes, "Medical and public health professionals at the New York City Department of Health were among the first to detect the AIDS infections, yet the city was slow to respond to the crisis.") The disease drew homosexuality out of the closet. By 2012, gay activists had persuaded the state legislature to legalize gay marriage in New York, which was viewed not only as a social milestone but as an economic development opportunity.

The city's health department still describes New York as the nation's epicenter of HIV/AIDS. Today about one hundred thousand New Yorkers are living with the disease, which is now a chronic illness thanks to advanced medicines. It remains the third leading cause of death for New Yorkers between the ages of forty-five and fifty-four (after cancer and heart disease). A decade ago, the death rate was more than 21 per 100,000 New Yorkers. Today it is about one-third that.

•92•

Casita

At Home in the Barrio

Puerto Ricans migrated to New York beginning in the nineteenth century, then again after the Spanish-American War in 1898. They were granted U.S. citizenship in 1917, and by the 1950s, a sluggish economy and a search for jobs, coupled with the advent of air travel, triggered the great migration to New York. Tens of thousands of Puerto Ricans were pouring into New York annually (an estimated 75,000 in 1953 alone), establishing barrios in Spanish Harlem, the Lower East Side, and Williamsburg, Brooklyn, where bodegas, *piragueros* (shaved-ice vendors) and casitas—small cottages that evoked the look and feel of Puerto Rico—proliferated by the 1970s.

Transplants celebrated their literary, artistic, and musical culture—the budding Nuyorican movement—beginning with the first Puerto Rican Day Parade in 1958. The number of Puerto Ricans in the city peaked at more than 900,000, then began declining in 2000 with an exodus to the suburbs and a reverse migration to the island. (New York still has the largest Puerto Rican population of any city in the world.) Meanwhile, an influx from other parts of the Caribbean and Latin America shrank the Puerto Rican share of the city's Hispanic population. They remain the predominant group among Hispanics, outnumbering the growing Dominican population, now more than 600,000, and Mexicans, the fastest-growing group, with as many as 500,000 (followed by Ecuadorians and Colombians). By 2000, a surge in immigration and higher birthrates nudged Hispanic New Yorkers overall past blacks as the city's second-largest racial or ethnic group. Over 2.37 million Hispanic people live in New York City, more than in any other city in the United States. Spanish Harlem is becoming gentrified, as is the Lower East Side, which in Nuyorican (the local Latino vernacular), is "Loisaida." Popularized by the poet Bittman Rivas in 1974, the name became official when the city sanctioned Loisaida Avenue as another name for Avenue C in 1987.

One of the city's oldest and largest casitas, Rincon Criollo, has survived so long that it is almost eligible for landmark status (it has been proposed). Its legacy is preserved by the Rincon Criollo Cultural Center at 499 East 158th Street, and its biography recalls its role as an oasis "where people come to breathe culture that is not for sale," to gather, garden, stage community events, and perpetuate cultural and musical traditions (Rincon Criollo is credited with the emergence of the bomba and plena musical group Los Pleneros de la 21).

Rincon Criollo, which loosely means "down-home corner," originally opened a block away on a vacant lot owned by the Church of Saints Peter and Paul that was reclaimed when José Soto began cultivating vegetables and herbs through holes in the fence. When the lot was abandoned, neighbors built the one-story casita. Today, at their sixteen-square-foot clubhouse on a three-thousand-square-foot city-owned lot in the Melrose section, they boil cabbage on makeshift grills and press wine from grapes grown on a chain-link fence. Their move was financed in part by a grant from Nos Quedamos, a community group, whose executive director, Yolanda Gonzalez, said it's important for New Yorkers to know that casitas still exist. "It brings a light to what culture is to a community, why people came together, and why they stayed where they were," she said. "This is history that is not taught in textbooks."

·93·

Phantom's Mask

Regarding Broadway

New York theater dates back to the 1750s, when ballad operas and Shakespeare's plays were presented at venues downtown. Theater expanded in the 1820s to the Bowery, which became the city's first entertainment—in the loosest sense of the term—district. Niblo's Garden, a three-thousand-seat theater, opened at Broadway and Prince Street in 1829. Blackface minstrel shows proliferated, but race wasn't the only defining characteristic of the theater. In 1849, the Astor Place Riot pitted Irish immigrants against nativist Anglophiles in an outbreak of class warfare that left at least two dozen people dead. The proximate cause of the riot was the rivalry between two actors, one American and one British, but the underlying hostility was of Shakespearean proportions (and ultimately, after the state militia was summoned, led to the formation of an armed city police force).

The theater's history since then has been relatively bloodless, but no less melodramatic, studded with names like Booth, Barrymore, Berlin, Shubert, Rodgers and Hammerstein, Robbins, Sondheim, Lloyd Webber, and others who defined Broadway, including the largely forgotten Charles Frohman, a prolific producer of more than seven hundred shows, whose own final act—he died in 1915 when the *Lusitania* was torpedoed—was suitably theatrical. Broadway was dubbed "The

Great White Way" (accounts differ as to whether the name was inspired by the bright untinted lights or a 1902 snowstorm) early in the twentieth century, when a critical mass of new venues established Times Square as the latest theater district.

Definitions of firsts in the theater are fluid. Musicals began with *The Black Crook* as early as 1866, although some experts date them to Jerome Kern and Guy Bolton's *Very Good Eddie* in 1915 and, most notably, to Jerome Kern and Oscar

Hammerstein II's *Show Boat* in 1927. The "first" show produced by blacks and starring black actors is said to have been Eubie Blake and Noble Sissel's *Shuffle Along* in 1921. The American Theater Wing awarded its first Tonys (named for Antoinette Perry, the actress and director) in 1947, the same decade that off-Broadway productions took hold.

No production ran as long, made as much money, or attracted audiences as successfully as *The Phantom of the Opera,* by Andrew Lloyd Webber, which was imported from London and opened in New York in 1988. On January 9, 2006, it overtook *Cats* to become the longest-running Broadway musical (7,486 performances to that date alone). The Phantom's mask became a global icon.

According to the producers association, almost twelve million theatergoers attended Broadway shows in 2012–13, including forty-six new productions—more than the combined attendance for Mets, Yankees, Rangers, Islanders, Knicks, Nets, Liberty, Giants, Jets, and Devils games. The Broadway League estimates that theater generates $11 billion for the city's economy, (ticket sales constitute over $1 billion—top ticket price for *Phantom,* $200; average price, $90) and supports more than 80,000 local jobs.

Because of policies initiated by Mayors Koch, Dinkins, and Giuliani, a resurgent Times Square came to symbolize a city that broke population and tourism records. In 2013 the city drew more than fifty-four million visitors.

·94·

Con Ed Chimney

Letting Off Steam

New Yorkers typically don't know much about what goes on beneath the city's streets until it bubbles to the surface. One exception is those orange-and-white funnel stacks belching steam from Consolidated Edison Co. manholes. The online magazine *Slate* described them rather glamorously, invoking "Brigitte Bardot clutching a Gauloise." To others, they nostalgically evoke the perpetual Camel smoker who famously blew perfect rings from a billboard above Times Square. To yet others, the temporary candy-striped chimneys resemble the Cat in the Hat's headgear.

Steam is one of those forces of nature that people tend to take for granted or associate with a kettle, but it has played a vital role in New York's development. Robert Fulton and his paddle wheeler *Clermont* heralded the shift from sail to steam on rivers and oceans, a shift that, by delivering reliable service not dependent on the whim of the winds, helped seal the city's preeminence as a port.

For over 125 years, underground steam has played a significant part in heating and, more recently, cooling some of New York's biggest buildings. That process began with the New York Steam Co. in 1882, servicing the United Bank Building at Broadway and Wall from a plant bounded by Cortlandt, Dey, Greenwich, and

Washington Streets at the future site of the World Trade Center (when the plant was built, its 225-foot-high smokestack was the second tallest structure in Lower Manhattan, after the spire of Trinity Church). The company grew into the largest such commercial enterprise anywhere.

Con Ed, which fully acquired New York Steam in 1954, supplies steam in Manhattan south of Ninety-Sixth Street on the West Side and Eighty-Ninth Street on the East Side to properties that include Rockefeller Center, the Empire State Building, the Chrysler Building, Grand Central Terminal, the United Nations headquarters, the World Trade Center, the Metropolitan Museum, and eighteen hundred other customers. The economics are simple: a few large steam boilers servicing multiple customers are cheaper than installing, operating, and servicing boilers in every building. The company delivers steam through 105 miles of mains and pipes serviced by 3,000 manholes.

Most of the steam stays underground. It's visible at street level when vapor escapes from manholes and water comes in contact with steam, sometimes because of leaks. The orange-and-white stacks are placed pending repairs so drivers' views are not obstructed by steam and so pedestrians aren't burned (the steam is delivered at a temperature of 358 degrees). Steam is used to cool buildings by driving turbines that help circulate a refrigerant or boil off water for evaporation.

Except for the chimneys, which contain the escaping steam, most of what goes on below ground is largely invisible—the cables, gas, water, electricity, sewers, and telephone conduits that course below streets and sidewalks, subways, and vehicular tunnels excepted.

·95·

New Year's Ball

Something About Eves

The globe is divided into two dozen standard time zones, but for more than a century, New York's Times Square has defined New Year's eve to the world.

The New York Times might have been caricatured as "the old gray lady" for her dense news columns and prim reporting, but the newspaper was more famous for fireworks and the illuminated ball that descended every December 31 from its trapezoidal headquarters to usher in the New Year. Since 1907 (except during wartime blackouts in 1942 and 1943), millions of revelers shivered in Times Square (the coldest New Year's temperature was 1 degree in 1917), listened on radio, or watched on television or the Internet as the last seconds of the old year were ebulliently counted down.

"Every morn is a new beginning, every day is the world made new," Adolph Ochs, the paper's publisher, proclaimed. On no day was that more true than when a new year was about to begin. Newspapers were known as the second hand of history, so it seemed perfectly in keeping with the tenor of the *Times*, a recent arrival in what had been called Longacre Square at West Forty-Second Street, that the paper would not only blaze election night results through multicolored beacons pointing in different directions, but also would celebrate the pivotal moment

on New Year's Eve. The festivities began with fireworks on December 31, 1903 (later, they were complemented on radio and television by Guy Lombardo's orchestra at the Waldorf-Astoria and Robert Trout narrating on CBS from the Astor Hotel marquee or Dick Clark at his *American Bandstand*).

Time balls—spheres lowered from poles to permit synchronization of clocks and watches and navigational chronometers—were commonplace in the nineteenth century, so what would become the *Times's* annual publicity stunt was a natural outgrowth of this practice. It would soon displace other traditional New Year's Eve celebrations in the city, the most heavily attended at Trinity Church downtown.

Ochs hired Artkraft Strauss to design the first iron and wood ball, which weighed 700 pounds, measured 5 feet in diameter, and was festooned with 100 25-watt bulbs. Later incarnations became more elaborate. A second version debuted in 1920, followed by a third in 1955 (decorated in the 1980s as a red and green Big Apple). A fourth, weighing in at 1,070 pounds, framed by 504 Waterford crystal triangles and illuminated by 600 bulbs, spinning mirrors, and strobes, was designed to mark the millennium. A fifth, weighing 1,212 pounds, 6 feet across, and sparkling with 9,567 bulbs, was introduced to celebrate the centennial of the first ball drop and herald 2008 (the ball was used only on December 31, 2007, and is on permanent display at the Times Square Museum and Visitor Center).

The *Times* moved from its iconic headquarters at the Crossroads of the World to nearby Eighth Avenue in 2007. Much of Times Square, still home to the Theater District, has been transformed into a vibrant pedestrian mall. The ball-dropping tradition continues, bigger than ever. The latest version, which debuted on December 31, 2008, is a mammoth icosahedral geodesic sphere that weighs 11,875 pounds and is 12 feet in diameter. Nowadays, the weatherproof ball remains visible year-round atop One Times Square.

·96·

Wired

The Terminal Was the Start

In 1982 Michael R. Bloomberg, a laid-off investment banker, invented his eponymous computer terminal. That little beige box soon made him the richest and most powerful man in New York. By affirming his faith in scientific solutions, it also helped deliver the city into the twenty-first century, through devices ranging from the expansion of the CompStat tactical crime-fighting program to the 311 telephone complaint and service system, and encouraged the evolution of Silicon Alley.

Since the nineteenth century, doomsayers have predicted that one scientific breakthrough after another—from the Atlantic cable to the telephone, from television to jet travel—would topple New York as the nation's financial and cultural capital. Instead, a resilient city that thrives on reinventing itself transformed a potential threat into an opportunity. Milliseconds are vital to global trading, but nothing beats face-to-face contact to foster innovation. A wired city provided both.

In under three decades, more than 300,000 subscribers were paying as much as $24,000 a year per terminal to access Bloomberg's real-time financial data, trading platform, and news feeds. His privately held company generated enough profit to make him a billionaire. Like a modern Medici, he invested a mind-boggling

$268 million of his personal fortune into three mayoral campaigns. (During that twelve-year period, his net worth ballooned from about $5 billion to over $30 billion.) No other New York mayor had approached that level of financial clout since William R. Grace, the city's first Irish-Catholic mayor, who left a fortune of $25 million (over $600 million in today's dollars) when he died in 1904.

Bloomberg's philosophy: The perfect is the enemy of the good. In other words, just do it. "Our product," he said, "would be the first in the investment business where normal people without specialized training could sit down, hit a key, and get an answer to financial questions, some of which they didn't even know they should ask." In the decades since, he said, two constants endured: "the need for information; and the users of data, with their bravery, jealousy, adventurousness and fear of the new."

Those constants spawned ubiquitous iPhones and tablets, of course, as well as Bloomberg terminals. But they also transformed obsolete communication hubs (such as 111 Eighth Avenue, 32 Avenue of the Americas, and 60 Hudson Street) into giant Internet gateways. Underground conduits hidden beneath nondescript Empire City subway manholes that date from the nineteenth century became futuristic fiber-optic highways pulsing with messages at nearly the speed of light.

·97·

Jar of Dust

An American Tragedy

September 11, 2001, began beautifully, a stunning late-summer morning. It was primary election day in New York, and voters were choosing a successor to Mayor Rudolph Giuliani. He was barred by newly imposed term limits from running again, but even more constrained by his own unpopularity as a scold, despite demonstrating that New York was indeed governable, and effecting remarkable reductions in crime.

Within 104 minutes that morning, beginning at 8:46 A.M., two planes, each hijacked by five Islamic terrorists, toppled both towers of the World Trade Center (two other planes were commandeered; one rammed the Pentagon, and the second crashed in Pennsylvania, apparently en route to a target in Washington). Nearly three thousand people died in the worst single foreign assault on American soil (it was the second attack on the World Trade Center; terrorists had detonated a truck bomb in a basement garage in 1993). Officially, including the passengers and crew of the two airliners, 2,753 people were killed after the towers collapsed. It was also the nation's deadliest tragedy for firefighters. Makeshift memorials sprouted everywhere, as did walls of handmade and photocopied missing posters desperately appealing for information on the whereabouts of friends, colleagues, and family members.

Cleanup of the site was completed the following May, after hundreds of thousands of tons of debris were removed. Beyond the horrific loss of life, the attack inflicted incalculable and enduring economic and personal damage. Stock exchanges closed for days. Transportation was curtailed, from a temporary freeze on air travel to years of subway service disruptions. Jobs were lost. Small businesses and residents were displaced. Exposure to toxic debris produced long-term illnesses. Politically, Giuliani's performance in the aftermath of the attack burnished his sagging reputation. His endorsement of Michael R. Bloomberg cinched the mayoral election for the billionaire businessman, who was viewed as most capable of perpetuating the best parts of Giuliani's legacy.

The loss of life was memorialized in the Municipal Art Society's annual Tribute in Light—searchlights evoking the Twin Towers. The buildings' footprints were filled with contemplative reflecting pools, and an underground memorial to the victims was constructed. A new World Trade Center was built—at a symbolic 1,776 feet to the top of its spire—and downtown was revitalized with new buildings and a population boom, at least until Hurricane Sandy inflicted heavy flood damage eleven years later.

The attack lingered indelibly in words and images, including a snapshot by John Labriola, an employee of the Port Authority of New York and New Jersey, which built the sixteen-acre site beginning in 1966. (1.2 million cubic yards of excavated earth expanded Manhattan's borders into the Hudson to create the Battery Park City residential complex.) Labriola's photograph depicted a young fireman climbing the stairs in the north tower. Labriola's words were equally poignant: "The one conclusion I came to on 9/11 is that people in the stairwell were in a state of grace. They helped each other. They didn't panic. Most people are basically good. I knew this, with certainty, because I had gone through the crucible. What a great example people left: be selfless, help the person around you, and get through it."

The historic attack defined a decade and left a grim legacy that took many forms. Among them was a jar of dust collected by New-York Historical Society curators at Ground Zero.

·98·

Domino Sign

Making It

It's another sign of times gone by, the Domino Sugar Refinery, which dates to a complex originally built in 1856. A little over a decade after it opened, the plant was processing half the sugar used in the United States. Today it's a derelict hulk, a relic of the city's unrivaled standing in the nineteenth and early twentieth centuries as the industrial capital of the country. As recently as 1950, the city still boasted more than a million manufacturing jobs. Today only about 150,000 New Yorkers work in manufacturing (although more than 300,000 work in what the census defines as production, transportation, and moving material). According to the Bureau of Labor Statistics' narrower definition, the number slipped below 100,000 in 2007 for the first time in over a century.

While clothing, chemicals, metal products, furniture, and processed foods are among the major manufactures, New York companies make everything from pianos (the old Steinway plant in Astoria, Queens) to landing gear for spacecraft (Vahl in Brooklyn). While waste paper is tops in tonnage, chocolate leads in the specialty-food category and cut diamonds in the value of exports. Old loft spaces are being converted into incubators for 3-D printing plants.

"The tendency of people to attract more people is the central idea of urban economics, and nowhere is that idea more obvious than in America's largest city," the Harvard urbanologist Edward Glaeser has written. "New York's initial advantage as a port then attracted manufacturing and services to cater to the mercantile firms and to take advantage of their low shipping costs."

Sugar manufacturing began as early as 1730, when Nicholas Bayard opened the first refinery, followed by the Havemeyers in the nineteenth century. Refining emerged as a direct by-product of trade with the West Indies. New York flour was shipped south, and raw sugar returned as cargo. Transportation, skilled labor, and fuel costs were lower in New York. Moreover, refining had to be done closer to the point of consumption to keep the sugar crystals from coalescing. New York, given its central location, also provided economies of scale. Sugar was the biggest industry in Brooklyn by 1870 and remained New York City's second largest through 1900.

After producing as much as three million pounds of sugar a day (the Domino-shaped rectangular cuboids were introduced as a marketing innovation in 1920), the refinery on Kent Avenue in Williamsburg was shuttered in 2004 after a long strike that idled mostly immigrant workers from Jamaica, Italy, and Eastern Europe. The only visible reminder of a vast industrial might is the Domino logo. Like the giant Silvercup and Pepsi signs, it is not an official landmark, though each suggests the physical transformation of the post-industrial waterfront. Silvercup Bakery in Long Island City, Queens, closed in 1975, but Silvercup film and television studios, based in the old factory, keeps its sign lighted and its name alive. The red neon Pepsi sign has illuminated the East River waterfront in Hunters Point, Queens, since 1936, when it stood atop a bottling plant that has been displaced by pricey high-rise apartments. The forty-foot-high neon Domino sign on the abandoned refinery in Williamsburg, Brooklyn, is supposed to be preserved once the site metamorphoses into offices and apartments.

· 99 ·

Stuyvesant Yearbook

The Asian Ascendancy

Mark another notch for ethnic succession. When City Councilman John C. Liu of Queens was elected comptroller in 2009, it was the first time an Asian-American had won citywide office in New York. Liu, who was born in Taiwan and moved to the United States when he was five, was the first city councilman of Asian descent when he was elected to that office in 2001. In 2012 Grace Meng, another Taiwanese-American born to immigrant parents, won a Democratic congressional nomination in Queens and became the city's first Asian-American member of Congress.

New York remains an immigrant mecca. Today more than three million, or almost 40 percent, of New Yorkers were born abroad, rivaling the record proportions at the beginning of the twentieth century. More than one in four of these immigrants arrived since 2000. New York has more persons of West Indian ancestry than any city outside the West Indies and more Dominicans than any city except Santo Domingo. New York has the largest ethnic Chinese population outside of Asia (about 500,000), including growing Chinatowns in Queens and Brooklyn. (Among U.S. cities, San Francisco is second, with about 175,000.) While Chinese predominate among Asians in New York, the city is also home to 230,000 Indians, 100,000 Koreans, 82,000 Filipinos, 50,000 Bangladeshis, and 45,000 Pakistanis.

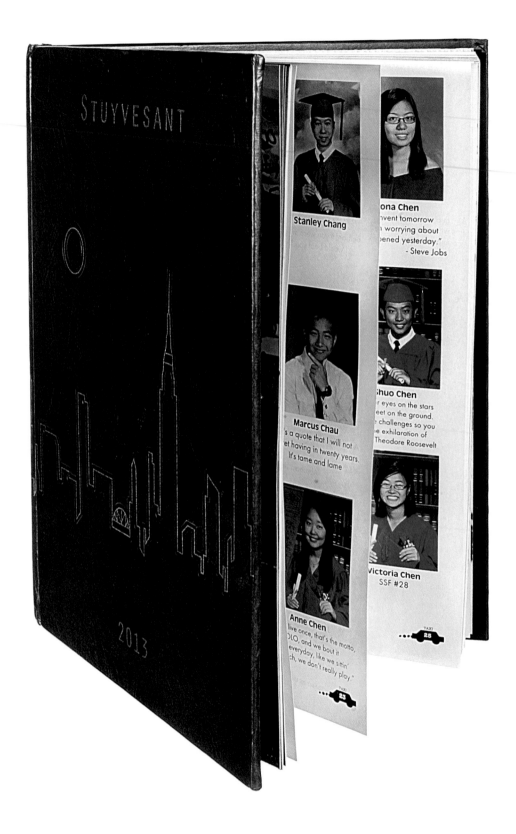

Stanley Chang

...ona Chen
...nvent tomorrow
...n worrying about
...pened yesterday."
- Steve Jobs

Marcus Chau
...s a quote that I will not
...et having in twenty years.
It's tame and lame

...Shuo Chen
...r eyes on the stars
...eet on the ground.
...e challenges so you
...e exhilaration of
...Theodore Roosevelt

Anne Chen
...live once, that's the motto,
...OLO, and we bout it
...everyday, like we sittin'
...ch, we don't really play."

Victoria Chen
SSF #28

The first modest wave of Chinese immigration, around 1870, ended abruptly with the Chinese Exclusion Act of 1882. Immigration surged after the lifting of quotas in 1965. Asians are the fastest-growing racial group in the city. As recently as 1990, there were fewer than 500,000, concentrated in Manhattan's Chinatown, and accounting for under 7 percent of the city's population. Today the more than one million Asians comprise almost 13 percent of New Yorkers, including nearly one in four residents of Queens, where half the city's Asian population lives. They constitute a majority in a number of neighborhoods (including Queens Community District 7, which encompasses Flushing, Whitestone, and College Point). Even on Staten Island, typically more resistant to racial and ethnic change, the share of Asians today is higher than it was citywide in 1990.

While black and Hispanic students constitute about seven in ten students citywide, the faces in the yearbooks of specialized high schools, such as Stuyvesant, are nearly all Asian or white non-Hispanic. Asians are succeeding aging non-Hispanic whites in swaths of Brooklyn, including Bensonhurst (where the Asian population on some blocks doubled over the last decade) and in Whitestone, Fresh Meadows, and Oakland Gardens, in northeastern Queens.

New York began the second decade of the twenty-first century with another growth spurt, adding more people than any other city in the country and, for the first time in decades, outpacing population gains in its neighboring suburbs. Much of that growth was fueled by immigrants and their children.

· 100 ·

Charlotte Street House

The Bronx, Yes, Thonx

Charlotte Street is a few miles from Yankee Stadium, where Howard Cosell intoned, when a derelict public school caught fire just before Game 2 of the 1977 World Series: "There it is, ladies and gentlemen, the Bronx is burning." Charlotte Street became an apocalyptic paradigm of urban decay and an obligatory campaign stop—"the worst slum in America," Jimmy Carter called it when he visited that year. Ronald Reagan later said it looked worse than London after the Blitz. But like the proverbial phoenix, Charlotte Street, the core of a South Bronx cancer spread by arson and neglect, was revived through an expensive public-private partnership that symbolized government intervention at its best. "I'm impressed by the spirit of hope and determination by the people to save what they have," Carter said during his surprise visit, and after touring a moonscape of rubble, he ordered his housing secretary to "see what areas can still be salvaged."

An urban embarrassment was transformed into a twenty-acre model of renewal and renaissance in a borough where, for the first time after decades of abandonment by anyone who could afford to leave, median household income is slowly increasing and the population is on the rise. "If you want to make an argument that government can work on a large scale and accomplish remarkable tasks, this is it,"

Marc Jahr, former president of the city's Housing Development Corporation, said of the Bronx renaissance.

The nadir of the South Bronx (and perhaps the city itself) may have been 1977. For all the Bronx cheers that mayoral third terms typically deserve, it was thanks to Edward Koch's collaboration with Fernando Ferrer, the Bronx borough president, that Charlotte Street and environs were revived. In the following decade, an estimated $1 billion investment in the South Bronx produced 19,000 apartments, 2,500 new homes (including the 92 on Charlotte Street), and the transformation of abandoned buildings into habitable multifamily homes. "There has been no more dramatic revival of a community in the country," said Paul S. Grogan, president of the Local Initiatives Support Corp., which helps local housing groups.

The Charlotte Street ranch houses cost about $110,000 to build and sold for about half that amount (subsidized by federal, city, and private funds). Even then, six hundred applications poured in during the first three weeks, mostly from working families in the Bronx. Among them was one from Joe Santiago, a maintenance man at New York University, who grew pears, peaches, and apples in the backyard of a home that, by the 1990s, he described as "like a piece of the country inside the city. It's not like the '60s or the '70s." Not long after, when former mayor Koch toured the site of his greatest triumph, he was offered a melon-size tomato by one homeowner. "Look at that," he declared with characteristic élan. "You can't beat this. This is like living in Great Neck."

Charlotte Street evolved from the poster neighborhood for urban decay to a suburban enclave where pleasure boats are parked in driveways, satellite dishes protrude from roofs, and front yards are bordered by meticulously maintained ornamental wrought-iron gates. "While its low density may no longer seem the most productive use of urban land in the context of affordable housing needs," a report by preservationists notes, "from a historic perspective the development's pivotal influence in reversing the borough's decline renders Charlotte Gardens an important historic district candidate." In 2012 Joe Santiago sold the five-bedroom, three-bath home at 1545 Charlotte Street, which he bought for $53,000 and retired to Florida. The price? A cool $300,000. (At the height of the real estate market, five years earlier, a house on the next block had sold for $430,000.)

·101·

Madonna

Another Phoenix from the Ashes

It was nicknamed a "superstorm," and it lived up to its reputation so fiercely that Sandy was retired from the pool of storm names bestowed by the World Meteorological Organization. Hurricane Sandy, which struck just before Halloween in 2012, was the second costliest storm in United States history ($68 billion), the biggest recorded Atlantic hurricane (spanning 1,100 miles), and took more than forty lives in New York City alone. Flooding shut down mass transit, created gasoline shortages, rendered homes uninhabitable, collapsed building facades, and released billions of gallons of raw sewage into waterways. A 13.88-foot-high storm surge from New York Bay inundated Lower Manhattan, crippling transportation, power supplies, and communications for months (the New York Stock Exchange closed for two consecutive days because of weather, the first time since the Blizzard of 1888).

Disaster officials described the storm as worse than Hurricane Katrina, which devastated New Orleans in 2005; than the September 20, 1938, hurricane, which soaked the city with five inches of rain; and than a September 3, 1821, storm, which fused the Hudson and East Rivers in Lower Manhattan.

Sandy struck a city with a greater population density and a more developed beachfront than ever in its history, which meant there was more to damage, particularly in flood-prone sections of Staten Island, Brooklyn, and Queens. In Breezy Point, Queens, a fire obliterated 111 homes, many of them converted summer bungalows, and damaged nearly two dozen others. Jamaica Bay and the Atlantic Ocean converged across the Rockaway Peninsula, and until the waters receded, frustrated firefighters were unable to reach the blaze, which spread to six alarms by 11:00 P.M. on October 29. Fire may seem an incongruous consequence of a hurricane, but officials later said it began when seawater came in contact with household electrical wires. The five-hundred-acre private beachfront community on the

western tip of the peninsula is heavily populated by the families of police officers, firemen, and other civil servants, and has the second-highest concentration of Irish-Americans (it is known locally as the Irish Riviera) of any zip code in the country.

Fittingly, the most visible survivor of the fire was a three-foot-high masonry Madonna, "a triumph of faith in the midst of the ashes," as Monsignor Michael J. Curran explained it. The Madonna had belonged to Charlie Shannon, who had bought the bungalow at 2 Gotham Walk on the corner of Oceanside Avenue in 1929 for his wife and seven children. Only one of the seven had children of his own, and in 2006 his granddaughter Regina Bodnar inherited a version of the house that her aunt and uncle rebuilt. Her aunt Mary placed the Madonna just outside, Bodnar recalled, "and each morning Breezy neighbors stopped to say a prayer by the statue, and the young children and grandchildren of our neighbors waved and said, 'Hi Mary!' as they raced by."

The statue was neither consumed by the fire nor toppled by the storm surge (it was not cemented in place but stood precariously on its own in the sea grass). Does Bodnar believe in miracles? She's not sure, but said that somehow her neighbors and rescue workers "were miraculously protected from serious injury and loss of life." Monsignor Curran, the pastor of St. Thomas More Church, took custody of the Madonna after the storm subsided. "It will be a symbol of the suffering but also of our rise from the ashes," he said. "It will be a symbol of what we've been through, but also of our resurrection. It will be a reminder that for all the property we lost, God never left."

• Epilogue •

Oh, what we left out! Don't ask. But please, do tell.

Our first incarnation of *Objects,* published in *The New York Times* on September 12, 2012, prompted hundreds of suggestions from readers and a few complaints about both objects we included and many that were omitted. Now it's your turn.

Other readers recommended Bella Abzug's hat, hearty helpings of ethnic food, a Playbill or theater marquee to epitomize Broadway, a Stork Club ashtray as symbolic of the Roaring Twenties (when liquor was officially banned but smoking was allowed). What about Miss Rheingold and Miss Subways, some artifact from Tin Pan Alley, and the *Alice in Wonderland* statue at the model sailboat pond in Central Park?

Mayor Bill de Blasio nominated the striking photographs in Jacob Riis's 1890 exposé of tenement squalor, *How the Other Half Lives,* which seared the conscience of New Yorkers to inspire reform. Former mayor Michael Bloomberg concurred in our choice of Emma Lazarus's sonnet, which he said evokes immigration, marriage equality, freedom of religion, and "the values that define New York City." Louise Mirrer, president of the New-York Historical Society, proposed the Sanitation Department's mechanical street sweeper, which today sends motorists scurrying to move their parked cars. Kenneth T. Jackson, the Columbia professor and historian of New York, suggested a mangled window blind that blew free from the World Trade Center and landed in the cemetery of St. Paul's Chapel across the street. Neil MacGregor, director of the British Museum, nominated Louis Lozowick's 1925 cityscape from an elevated train, which, he said, "captures both the geometry and the kineticism of art deco New York."

Several other suggestions were truly inspired. One reader proposed the one-by-three-inch Delaney card, a visual seating device invented by a Bronx public school teacher that "held the power of life and death over a student." What about the inflatable rat perched menacingly at non-union construction sites, an unwitting symbol of how much the air has gone out of organized labor. How about a metal sidewalk subway ventilation grate (there'll be no new ones on the Second Avenue line or the No. 7 extension to replicate that memorable Marilyn Monroe moment from *The Seven Year Itch*). A cover of *The Crisis* magazine, published by the NAACP and edited by W. E. B. Du Bois. A Macy's Thanksgiving Parade balloon. The original edition of *Ms.* magazine. Louis Armstrong's trumpet. Alfred E. Smith's brown derby and the sheet music to his campaign theme song, "The Sidewalks of New York." Egbert Viele's 1865 topographical map of Manhattan, which charted streams and the original coastline and which today's civil engineers still depend on. A jukebox that played opera music at a hamburger joint in the Times Square subway station in the 1950s.

The list goes on. A Henry Ward Beecher sermon. A pigeon. A 1955 Brooklyn Dodgers World Series banner. And many, many more.

These 101 objects offer just a glimpse, an illustrated matchbook to ignite your imagination. As O. Henry said of New York, "It'll be a great place if they ever finish it." Any history of New York is by nature organic; it grows with time. It can never be finished. Today the city is the biggest it has ever been. The possibilities are boundless.

Let the parlor game begin. Send me your suggestions at ObjectsOfNYC@gmail.com.

• Acknowledgments •

In Alan Bennett's play *The History Boys,* one of the students is asked to define history, to which he replies, more or less, it's just one damn thing after another. For a daily journalist, it's that, only faster. The pace is set by the unforgivingly swift second hand of history. At *The New York Times,* we strive to provide context, to turn history into news, to make it resonate in today's headlines, and to fit current events into historical perspective. The *Times* generously indulges my passion, and I'm appreciative. Books offer an even more capacious platform on which to experiment and broaden my reach. This one was inspired by a collaborative project between the British Museum and the British Broadcasting Corp. Thanks, especially, to the museum's research manager, Dr. Jeremy D. Hill, for his helpful suggestions.

Valuable insights, as always, were provided by Professors Kenneth T. Jackson, Mike Wallace, and Edwin Burrows; Robert Weible, the New York State historian; Louise Mirrer and Valerie Paley of the New-York Historical Society; Susan Henshaw Jones and Sarah Henry of the Museum of the City of New York; Harold Holzer of the Metropolitan Museum of Art; Ellen Futter of the American Museum of Natural History; Thomas Lannon of the New York Public Library; Eileen Flannelly, deputy commissioner of the New York City Department of Records, and Leonora Gidlund and Ken Cobb of the Municipal Archives; Richard Lieberman of the La Guardia and Wagner Archives; borough historians Michael Miscione of Manhattan, Lloyd Ultan of the Bronx, Jack Eichenbaum of Queens, Ron Schweiger of Brooklyn, and Thomas Matteo of Staten Island; Dorothy Dougherty of the National Archives and Records Administration; New York State Historical Association; the Organization of American Historians; the Center for Jewish History; the Transit Museum; the Ellis Island Immigration Museum; the Tenement Museum; the African Burial Ground National Monument; the Bowery Boys, Ephemeral New York; the Coney Island History Project; the Baseball Hall of Fame; the Wildlife Conservation Society; St. Paul's Parish; City College of New York; the National Park Service; the Apollo Theater; the New York Philharmonic Archives; and the Landmarks Preservation Commission.

Others who generously weighed in include Ralph Appelbaum, Della Britton Baeza, Hilary Ballon, Renee Barnes, Thomas Bender, Andrew Blum, Arthur Browne, Ann Buttenwiser, Jeff Byles, Robert A. Caro, Daniel Czitrom, Dorothy Dougherty, Pearl Duncan, Nina Flowers, Ann Foulkes, Harvey Frommer, Roberta Gratz, Timothy Gilfoyle, John Herzog, Tony Hiss, Eric Homberger, Sandy Hornick, Jay Hershenson, Steven Jaffe, Ben Kafka, Lisa Keller, Gerald Koeppel, William Kornblum, Roberto Lebron, the Reverend Joseph McShane, Barry Moreno, Jonathan Pace, Lisandro Perez, James Sanders, Luc Sante, Nicholas Sbordone, Jeff Sotzing, Benjamin Swett, Tony Tung, Vito Turso, David Walsh, Laura Washington, and Steve Zeitlin.

I'm always grateful for the encouragement, guidance, and support of my editors and colleagues at *The New York Times,* especially Amy Virshup, Blake Wilson, Diego Ribadeneira, Carolyn Ryan, Wendell Jamieson, Michael Pollak, Charles Delafuente, and Phyllis Collazo. Thank you to the hundreds of *Times* readers who responded to our appeal to suggest objects. Niko Koppel masterfully and cheerfully wrangled all the photographs.

At Simon & Schuster, Bob Bender's enthusiasm and his judicious and meticulous judgment and editing made this book possible. Thanks, too, to the indispensable Johanna Li, Dan Cuddy, Joy O'Meara, and Kate Gales for their unstinting professionalism.

My agent, Andrew Blauner, once again fulfilled his confidence in me. I am enormously grateful for his faith and professionalism.

Thanks to Shelby White and to Mitch and Abby Leigh for their abiding support, generosity, and friendship. And to Paul Neuthaler, Dixie and Barry Josephson, Karen Salerno and Tom McDonald, and Mortimer Matz—you each know how much, in your own way, you helped.

Michael and Sophie, Will and Jessica, I am so proud of you. Marie, I love you and can never thank you enough.

• Photo Credits •

1. Niko Koppel
2. American Museum of Natural History
3. American Museum of Natural History/D. Finnin
4. Ozier Muhammad/*The New York Times*/Redux
5. National Archives of the Netherlands
6. New York State Archives
7. Collection of The New-York Historical Society
8. Julie Larsen Maher/Wildlife Conservation Society
9. Christian Hansen, Courtesy of The Staten Island Museum
10. Collection of The New-York Historical Society
11. National Park Service, Manhattan Historic Sites Archive
12. Collection of The New-York Historical Society
13. Leah Reddy/Trinity Wall Street
14. Tony Cenicola/*The New York Times*/Redux
15. General Services Administration
16. Courtesy of The New York Stock Exchange
17. Collection of The New-York Historical Society

18. Collection of The New-York Historical Society
19. American Antiquarian Society
20. Central Park Conservancy
21. Collection of The New-York Historical Society
22. Courtesy of Glens of Antrim Potatoes
23. Harris & Ewing Collection, The Library of Congress
24. Museum of the City of New York
25. ©2013 LegendaryAuctions.com
26. Otis Elevator Company
27. Collection of The New-York Historical Society
28. City College Library Archives/City University of New York
29. Robert Caplin for *The New York Times*/Redux
30. George Grantham Bain Collection/Library of Congress
31. Tony Cenicola/*The New York Times*/Redux
32. Collection of The New-York Historical Society
33. Collection of The New-York Historical Society
34. Nathaniel Brooks/*The New York Times*/Redux
35. Museum of the City of New York
36. Richard Perry/*The New York Times*/Redux
37. Tony Cenicola/*The New York Times*/Redux, Courtesy of The Demolition Depot
38. Ozier Muhammad/*The New York Times*/Redux
39. Niko Koppel
40. Sesame Workshop
41. Weegee (Arthur Fellig)/International Center of Photography/Contributor/Masters/Getty Images
42. Lisa Larson-Walker
43. Lisa Larson-Walker
44. Collection of The New-York Historical Society
45. Charles Denson Archive
46. Collection of The New-York Historical Society
47. Lisa Larson-Walker
48. Tony Cenicola/*The New York Times*/Redux

49. Yana Paskova/*The New York Times*/Redux
50. Neal Boenzi/*The New York Times*/Redux
51. U.S. Postal Service
52. Collection of The Newberry, Chicago
53. The Metropolitan Museum of Art
54. Courtesy of New York Transit Museum
56. Collection of The New-York Historical Society
57. Carol M. Highsmith America Collection/Library of Congress
58. Lisa Larson-Walker
59. Tony Cenicola/*The New York Times*/Redux
60. Christie's Images/The Bridgeman Art Library
61. New York City Housing Authority Artifacts Collection, The La Guardia and Wagner Archives at La Guardia Community College Publications, Inc./The City University of New York
62. Tony Cenicola/*The New York Times*/Redux
63. Columbia University Archives
64. © Woody Guthrie Publications, Inc.
65. WNYC Archive Collections
66. Damon Winter/*The New York Times*/Redux
67. The Commercial Appeal
68. Courtesy of Steiner Sports
69. Julius and Ethel Rosenberg Case File, Courtesy of the National Archives and Records Administration
71. Marquee photo: The Leonard Bernstein Collection, Music Division, Library of Congress; letter: The Library of Congress
72. Bettmann/Corbis
73. Niko Koppel
74. National Baseball Hall of Fame Library
75. Christian Hansen, Courtesy of New York Transit Museum
76. Ed Sijmons
77. Mike Liebowitz/*The New York Times*/Redux
78. Librado Romero/*The New York Times*/Redux
79. Courtesy of Carson Entertainment Group

80. Tony Cenicola/*The New York Times*/Redux, Courtesy of The City Reliquary

81. Niko Koppel

82. Tony Cenicola/*The New York Times*/Redux

83. The Metropolitan Museum of Art

84. Collection of The New-York Historical Society

85. © GODLIS

87. Bill Stahl Jr./*New York Daily News* Archive, via Getty Images

88. Museum of Modern Art

89. Christian Hansen

90. Federal Reserve Bank of New York

91. Courtesy of William Dobbs

92. Librado Romero/*The New York Times*/Redux

93. Tony Cenicola/*The New York Times*/Redux

94. Niko Koppel

95. Richard Drew/Associated Press

96. Bloomberg LP

97. Collection of The New-York Historical Society

98. Tony Cenicola/*The New York Times*/Redux

100. Before: Edward Hausner/*The New York Times*/Redux; after: Ángel Franco/*The New York Times*/Redux

101. Kirsten Luce/*The New York Times*/Redux

DISCARD

974.7 ROBERTS

Roberts, Sam.
A history of New York
in 101 objects

METRO

R4001940693

METROPOLITAN
Atlanta-Fulton Public Library